PUB WA
A R O U
SOUTHAMPTON
AND CENTRAL HAMPSHIRE

PETER CARNE

Ensign

© **Peter Carne 1992**

First published in 1992
by **Ensign Publications**
a division of Hampshire Books Ltd.,
2 Redcar Street
Southampton SO1 5LL

a b c d

ISBN 185455 079 9

Publisher: *David Graves*
Maps: *Jack Street*
Cover Photos: *Terry Heathcote*
Book photos: *Peter Carne*
Cover Design: *The Design Lab*
Text pages: *The Precinct Press*
Printers: *The Romsey Printing Co., Chandlers Ford*

Also available in this series
Pub Walks in the New Forest
Pub Walks on the Isle of Wight (1993)
Pub Walks around Portsmouth
Pub Walks around Winchester (1992)
Pub Walks around Bournemouth and Poole (1993)
Pub Walks around Southampton and Central Hampshire

Walk   · **CONTENTS** ·   Page

· INTRODUCTION ·

The extra enjoyment that a good pub can bring to an outing on foot in rural Hampshire can be discovered on any one of the score of rambles suggested here. Besides being circular, of modest length and within easy reach of Southampton and surrounding areas either by car or by public transport, each of the walks starts and ends either at an individual pub or at a village or other locality where a choice of pubs is available.

Pubs mentioned have all been visited and the main points about them noted for your guidance. In most cases, publicans are happy for walkers who are also customers to use their car park — but most request that they be asked first, and this is a courtesy that should never be neglected. Some pubs do not have car parks, in which case alternative places to park are indicated in the text.

Walkers in Hampshire can enjoy an exceptional range of scenic routes in many different kinds of countryside. Hampshire County Council's rights of way and recreation department have been energetic in signposting paths, erecting new stiles wherever necessary and generally keeping an eye on the interests of those who walk for pleasure. They would like to hear of any problems caused by obstructions or other difficulties. The law requires farmers to reinstate paths promptly after ploughing and if you encounter a bull while walking a right of way, it should only be of a non-dairy breed and accompanied by cattle.

As well as these points to be watched out for, walking also imposes responsibilities on you the walker. Observe the country code at all times — in short, close all gates behind you, keep strictly to rights of way, do not damage property or leave litter and do not allow dogs to worry livestock or harass wildlife. Keep your dog on a lead or train it to walk to heel at all times.

As for what to wear while walking, except after periods of drought the most important item is waterproof footwear. Dress for warmth but do not overdo it. If the weather is warm but rain threatens, a pocketable plastic mac can be a safeguard against a soaking. A walking-stick or a thumbstick can be almost as useful as an extra leg, especially for coping with the odd patch of muddy going.

Pubs are liable to change hands or names or to close at fairly short notice. Likewise, road classifications have recently been in a considerable state of flux and bus services are prone to changes of route or operator.

Lastly, try to make friends wherever you walk!

PETER CARNE
May, 1992

A Forest Fringe and Shore Walk from near Fawley

WALK 1
2/3 hours
4 miles
Walk begins page 7

Background to the Walk

Until the early years of the 20th century the lower part of the area we now know as the Waterside, around Fawley, was sparsely populated and difficult of access. *The Victoria County History of Hampshire* mentions large tracts of uncultivated moorland, in the midst of which a small settlement of mud-walled dwellings, called 'Blackfields', had only recently been superseded by brick-built cottages. Such were the humble beginnings of Fawley's populous neighbour village, the Blackfield of today.

Fawley itself has a history going back at least to Norman times, when its Church of All Saints had its beginnings. Pleasingly added to over the centuries, the lovely old church became a bomb victim in World War II but was later faithfully restored. Another building of period interest is Fawley tide mill, confronting you when you arrive at Ashlett Creek. This is not so old as it looks, having been built in 1816. Its working life was short, apparently having ceased by 1890. In Edwardian times the building was relegated to use as a yacht store. It now functions as a club for oil refinery employees, the adjacent former mill pond being a sanctuary for birds.

Rural isolation was ended when in 1906 the London and South Western Railway Company introduced a bus service to Fawley from Totton. Nineteen years later came the railway, one of the last to be built in Britain. At first this had a sparse

Maps
Landranger 1:50,000
Sheet 196
Pathfinder 1:25,000
Sheet SU 40/50
Map Reference of
Start/Finish SU466032

How to get there
From the western end of Totton's southern bypass follow A326 and its continuation, B3053, from which turn left into Fawley village, towards the far end of which turn left again where a signpost points to Ashlett Creek. Carry on to the lane's end at the approach to Fawley's old tide mill. The pub lies to your left here with parking space is opposite. You can reach Fawley from Southampton by Solent Blue bus service X8, X9, 38 or 39, alight there and walk three-quarters of a mile to Ashlett Creek, or carry on for nearly a mile to Badminston Farm to begin and end your walk there.

Pub facilities
The Jolly Sailor.
*A Whitbread pub much
favoured by yachtsmen
and open 1100-2300
on weekdays (1200-
1500 and 1900-2230
on Sundays).*
*The restaurant is open
lunchtimes and eve-
nings except Sunday
and Monday evenings,
food orders being taken
between 1200-1400
and 1900-2100 with a
wide choice of starters,
main courses and
sweets. Salads,
sandwiches and
beverages are also on
the menu. Brews
include special offers
at reduced prices.
Walkers who use the
pub may also use the
large pub car park.*
*The pub fits in so
well with its creekside
environment that it is
tempting to tarry there
first and stoke up with
refreshment for the
walk. While doing so I
looked around the L-
shaped bar, with its
padded bench seats,
panelled ceiling and
pictures of ocean
greyhounds like
Titanic, Queen Mary,
her erstwhile compan-
ion Queen Elizabeth
and the present QE 2,
while making notes
about such matters as*

passenger service (later reduced still further) mainly to serve the needs of workmen, but its main traffic consisted of trains conveying products of the A.G.W.I. (Anglo-Gulf, West Indies Petroleum Corporation) depot at Fawley, established soon after World War I. Esso's arrival on the Waterside scene in 1951 presaged the creation of one of Europe's largest oil refineries, which helps to keep the branch railway in being as well as providing much local employment.

The placename 'Ashlett' probably has a simple explanation. 'Lett' has a modern counterpart in 'leat', meaning 'an open water-course conducting water to a mill etc', so here, one may guess, there was once a such a waterway beside which ash trees grew. Ashlett Creek, where this walk starts, is therefore something of a tautology — a needless duplication of names. It is studded in summer with pleasure craft which sit on the mud when the tide is low. At one time, or so I gather, a weekly barge brought coal and beer here from Southampton and conveyed passengers to and fro for a fare of sixpence (old money) return. In those days the creek was kept clear of silt by regular sluicing from the mill pond, just behind the adjacent old tide mill, unused now for more than a century.

Just down the coast, at Calshot, where a shingle spit separates Southampton Water from the Solent, Henry VIII had a castle built as one of a chain of defences against expected invasion from France. In our own century Royal Flying Corps, Royal Naval Air Service and finally Royal Air Force units were based here. Flying-boats were a local feature and, between the wars, the Schneider Trophy was raced for by flyers from Calshot. At the time of writing the old castle is headquarters for a sporting activities centre under county council control, the armed services having departed in April 1961.

Another feature seldom absent from view on this walk is Fawley Power Station, with its tall

that once, one cus-
tomer thinks, this
Waterside hostelry
was known as The
Jolly Roger. There is
nothing piratical today
about the bar prices, I
was assured.

To what was once a
local 'local' with strong
maritime connections,
high tides today bring
yachting customers in
droves every summer
weekend as potential
jolly sailors. Many
resort to the restau-
rant, with its menu, on
the day when I called,
of four starters and ten
main courses as well
as salads, side orders
and sandwiches. Food
is served from 1200-
1400 seven days a
week and from 1900-
2100 except on Satur-
days and Sundays.
The pub itself is open
from 1100-2300 on
weekdays and from
1200-1500 and 1900-
2230 on Sundays.
Children are allowed in
the restaurant area but
dogs are not. There is
additional parking
space opposite, while
just across the road
from the pub is a green
with tables and seats.

chimney dominating what, until well after World
War II, was an unspoilt rural scene. It is part of the
price we have to pay for all those amenities of life
we tend too often to take for granted but would be
hard put to it to do without!

Walk 1

Distance : Allow 2 to 3 hours for this 4-mile walk.

Follow a grass path around the walled upper end
of the creek to a swing-gate where you disregard
a left-pointing footpath sign and follow a track
leading right-ahead beside brambly rough pasture. Ignore a track that turns right to a gate and
carry on for a little way farther, watching out for
a narrow path that twists right-handed between
brambles. This leads to a staggered pedestrian
access to a meadow, the right-hand edge of which
you follow to its far corner. From this carry on
along a tree-bordered path with the perimeter
fence of Fawley Power Station to your left. Before
going farther, however, pause to look back across
meadow and saltmarsh to where Southampton
Water's shoreline retains a measure of rural charm,
with grass and trees protectively flanking the oil
refinery's approaches.

Ashlett Mill, last rebuilt in 1816.

Your grass-centred stony track matures into a metalled road. This leads to the power station's approach road, which you cross to follow a grass-and-gravel path which leads straight on. This in turn joins a gravel road by which you emerge past Badminston Farm, where a craft centre is now located. Refreshments, a licensed restaurant and a pizza bar I also saw advertised. Cross the main road here by a bus stop to follow metalled Badminston Lane. Hedged and bracken-bordered, this gives a view combining typically contrasting features of this area — oak-bordered pastures, a solitary cottage, all-pervading rural calm and, in the background, the inescapable, omnipresent Fawley oil complex rearing its sinister-looking hardware to bring you back to earth with a bump.

Disregard a crossing footpath and continue past the premises of an engineering firm. You then walk round a metal gate to follow a gravel track ahead, with a pig farm to your left. Within a few yards follow a path bending left through gorse bushes to join a track which you follow left-handed, with a high-fenced compound to your right. Where the latter ends, fork left and pass through a vehicle barrier to follow a track to the left of a fenced oakwood. At the next fork, with pine trees to your right, follow a gravel track ahead, past a tin-roofed dwelling — 'Cosy Corner' — to a stile beyond which you follow the right-hand edge of a pasture, with a pig farm now to your right.

Cross a further stile, with an oak and pine wood now to your left. Cross a woodland ride just ahead and then bear half-left to follow a path through hollies, bracken and tall pines, part of a wood called Spratsdown Plantation. Cross another ride to follow a fenced path ahead between two valley pastures and then continue through a pinewood, passing through a vehicle barrier to emerge on to Stanswood Lane. Cross this and pass through a second barrier preceding a parallel gravel lane. A metal stile ahead is followed by a fenced gravel path steering a way past sundry bungalows and former RAF married quarters to reach the main road

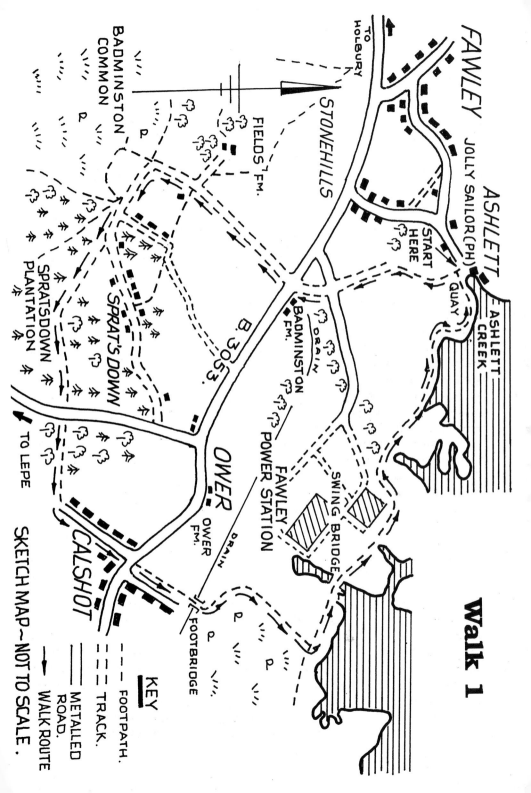

Walk 1

FAWLEY

ASHLETT

JOLLY SAILOR (PH)

STONEHILLS

TO HOLBURY

FIELDS FM.

BADMINSTON COMMON

START HERE

QUAY

ASHLETT CREEK

BADMINSTON FM.

DRAIN

SPRAT'S DOWN

SPRATSDOWN PLANTATION

B.3053

OWER

FAWLEY POWER STATION

SWING BRIDGE

DRAIN

OWER FM.

TO LEPE

CALSHOT

FOOTBRIDGE

KEY

- – – – – FOOTPATH.
- ▪ ▪ ▪ ▪ TRACK.
- ════ METALLED ROAD.
- → WALK ROUTE

SKETCH MAP ~ NOT TO SCALE.

View across Southampton Water from Ower Creek towards Hamble Estuary (and the site of Walk 20)

serving Calshot. Cross this and a stile on its far side to fol-low a signposted path along the right-hand edge of a scrubby pasture, with bungalows and wooden cabins lining a paddock to your right. After crossing a moist patch by means of a plank, you cross a stile by a World War II pillbox to follow a gravel path left-handed towards the chimney of Fawley Power Station.

Your gravel path soon veers right to skirt a flat and gravelly wilderness of grass and scattered bushes before joining the coastal footpath linking Calshot Spit and Ashlett. Follow this left-handed to cross by a security-fenced footbridge Ower Creek, which serves the adjacent power station as a cooling water intake. On its far side is a seat where I was glad to cool off myself while enjoying the view across creek and saltmarsh to Southampton Water's seaway, where a container ship loomed large and Isle of Wight ferries shuttled back and forth. For the next half-mile you skirt the perimeter of the power station complex, with chainlink fencing to your left and the spreading saltmarsh to your right. The shore path then leads you on through bushes, with fenced scrubland to your left. A walk-through 'stile' precedes more bushes. Where a gap in those to your right presents itself, turn right from the gravel path to reach the shore, alongside which your path veers left to skirt the premises of Esso Sailing Club and bring you back to the head of Ashlett Creek, The Jolly Sailor and your car.

Field Paths and Woodland Ways near West Tytherley

WALK 2
At least 3 hours
5 or 6 miles.
Walk begins page 13

Background to the Walk

Recorded as 'Tiderlei' in Domesday, Tytherley probably means 'young wood or clearing, where new growth is taking place': appropriate for a village still flanked by large woods and at one time lying within the old Royal Forest of Buckholt. North of the village there is still an area called Buckholt; the name probably means 'beechwood', but this now has very little woodland. Beyond the Wiltshire border, to the west, stretched Clarendon Forest, much of which is still heavily wooded.

One of the largest individual tracts of woodland, nearby Bentley Wood, once formed part of the Norman Court estate. A mediaeval owner was Roger Norman, who in 1334 acquired the West Bailey of Buckholt Forest by purchase and gave his estate the name. Norman Court mansion stands out prominently amid heavily wooded countryside as seen from the summit of Dean Hill, on the road between Whiteparish and West Dean — ideal for viewing the area traversed on this walk. The house dates from around 1730. Once owned by Thomas Baring of the banking family, in Edwardian times the house and estate were bought by Washington Singer of sewing machine fame. Following his death the estate was sold, much of the woodland being felled but later replanted by the Forestry Commission, who disposed of the major part to Bentley Wood Trust. The wood is now a nature reserve and Norman Court mansion is a school.

Maps
Landranger 1:50,000 Sheets 184 and 185 Pathfinder 1:25,000 Sheet SU 22/32 Map Reference of Start/Finish SU275300

How to get there
From Southampton follow A3024 to Redbridge interchange, then M271 and A3057 around Romsey to The Duke's Head pub at Greatbridge. Turn left there to follow B3084 and soon fork left from this for Awbridge and Lockerley where, after passing under the railway arch, keep right-ahead for East Tytherley and turn left there for West Tytherley, where you turn right at two successive junctions to reach The Black Horse on your left. Solent Blue buses on service 15 between Southampton and Romsey can be used to connect with bus

service 36 operated by Budden's Coaches of Romsey between that town and Salisbury, which is routed via West Tytherley.

Pub facilities
The Black Horse.

A village 'local' with an equally strong appeal to visitors, it serves excellent pub food, ranging from basket meals to full meals, lunchtimes and evenings, seven days a week. Walkers using the pub may use the pub car park provided they first obtain permission. Well-behaved dogs may be brought into the public bar.

One of West Tytherley's most striking period buildings is its pub. Mossy-tiled and with white-washed, creeper-clad walls, The Black Horse can have altered little in appearance since it first adorned the village, some 300 years ago. Pub walkers who will be using the pub may leave their vehicles here provided they ask the landlord first.

Exposed beams in the bar areas go with an open fireplace in which a woodburning stove adds a mildly modern

The towered church at West Tytherley dates from 1833, with a chancel added 44 years later. Pevsner and Lloyd sum it up as 'still entirely Georgian', while the Victoria County History refers to its three-light east window as being of 14th century style. The black marble font is early 13th century. Characterised by eyebrow windows peeping out from thatched or tiled gables, nearly all of West Tytherley's dwellings were once tied cottages occupied by Norman Court estate workers.

East Tytherley is another village whose inhabitants were nearly all employed by the local estate, in this case Lockerley Hall estate, owned from 1866 until recently by the Dalgety family. Surrounded by parkland and woods, Lockerley Hall was built in 1868-71 as an Elizabethan-style mansion on the site of a previous house called Oaklands, the onetime home of Sir William Fothergill Cooke, who helped invent the electric telegraph. Of a much older mansion, East Tytherley Manor House, no trace remains.

At the time of Domesday, East Tytherley manor is recorded as having been held by Alwi, son of Saulf. A 13th century lord of the manor, Michael de Columbars, made his mark by enclosing a sizeable chunk of it with a ditch and hedge to create a deer park. Remnants of the old boundary still surround farms and woods south-west of East Tytherley. The words 'Park Pale' in gothic text on the Pathfinder map show where it was.

A stubby steeple surmounts the 19th century tower of East Tytherley church, of which the main structure dates from around the middle of the 13th century. Original lancet windows in the chancel go with an arch from the same period, while on the south wall of the chancel is a representation of St. Peter, to whom the church is dedicated. When the present tower was being constructed a Henry III silver penny was discovered in the foundations.

The Black Horse, West Tytherley

Walk 2

Distance : Allow at least 3 hours for this walk of not quite 6 miles (not quite 5 miles by the shorter route).

Leaving The Black Horse pub at West Tytherley and its screening yew tree behind you on your right, walk south a little way along the main village road to a point where the school lies to your right and a footpath sign points left-handed. The path concerned leads left of a small building to where a plank bridge on your right precedes the approach to a private dwelling. Ignore this and fork left just short of the plank bridge to cross the first of four successive stiles, at each of which a plastic arrowhead shows the direction to be followed to keep correctly on course for the next stile.

Beyond stile number one you pass right-handed of a shallow, tree-fringed pond as indicated by the first arrowhead. Three pastures precede the fourth stile, after crossing which you follow the leftward edge of an arable field from which I disturbed a small covey of partridges — birds one sees all too seldom these days. After passing left of an open-

touch. Separate lounge and public bars are another traditional feature of what the landlord is happy to run as 'a proper English pub not spoilt by the brewery' — in this case, Whitbread. Three real ales include one 'guest' ale. Bar food can be ordered between 1200-1400 and between 1900-2200 (2130 on Sundays) seven days a week, pub opening times being 1100-1430 (until 1500 on Saturdays) and 1800-2300 on weekdays and between 1200-1500 and 1900-2230 on Sundays. The pub is noted for home-made curries, chillies, steak pies and fish dishes like stuffed trout and stuffed lemon sole. Family room caters for children as well as outside play area with climbing frames etc. A rear patio is popular in summer, while indoor facilities include a skittle alley and a pool table. Well-behaved dogs may be brought into the public bar.

East Tytherley Church

sided barn you con-
tinue along the left-
ward edge of a second
arable field, at the far
end of which you
cross a stile in a thick
hedgerow. You now
follow the hedged
leftward edge of an-
other arable field to a
further stile, beyond which your path has a fence to your left as you head
to another stile.

This brings you out on to a hedged green lane which you follow right-
handed. As you pass Strides Farm and its outbuildings, just ahead, the
lane becomes metalled and is flanked on the left by a thatched, white-
washed and timber-framed cottage as it leads on to join another lane at a
spot called Stony Batter. Just what the meaning of this name may be I have
never heard suggested.

Follow the last-mentioned lane right-handed to its junction with the road
linking the Tytherleys, West and East, which you follow left-handed,
passing Sopp's Farm on your right just before crossing a right-hand stile
by a footpath sign. Fenced on your right and hedged on your left, the path
you now follow skirts pony paddocks before crossing a hedged green lane
preceded and followed by further stiles. You now follow what I found to be
a very faintly defined path heading towards the far left corner of the arable
field directly beyond the green lane. After crossing another stile you follow
a gated track left-handed for a peep at East Tytherley church, directly
opposite what remains of the parkland timber which once graced the
surrounds of East Tytherley Manor House.

Leaving the church, retrace your steps along the hedged track to the gate
at its end, from which you follow a grass path left-handed with a railed
fence to your left. A stile and a plank bridge over a ditch precede your
approach to a kissing-gate beyond which you cross another hedged green
lane, then pass through a second kissing-gate. Your path now heads
diagonally right, away from the wood which lies to your left as you cross
arable land to a stile, beyond which you follow the edge of tree-sprinkled

Holbury Wood, deer fence and ladder

pasture with wood-land once more to your left. The scat-tered timber gives a decidedly park-like aspect to this area, which in fact lies within the bounds of East Tytherley's me-diaeval park whose 'pale' is still shown on the map as an earthwork relic from ancient times.

Pass through a gate at the end of the pasture to follow a track bridging a brook. At a track junction just ahead keep right, as directed by a footpath sign there, and carry on with a fir plantation to your right to reach a green track at right-angles to the one you have now been following. The shorter alternative return route here turns right to follow the green track between woods from which two emergent roe deer bobbed away ahead of me as I made my way along this section. As a 'right of way' open in theory to all traffic, this green way is much used by riders and therefore is apt to be muddy in parts, so boots and a stick are strongly advised here. The plantation to your right gives way to a screen of trees coinciding with the mediaeval park boundary, still discernible as a wasted bank and ditch running closely parallel with your route. The green track narrows to a path hemmed in by scrub on either hand and rising steadily to a point where you pass an isolated thatched dwelling on your right. You now reach and cross a metalled driveway to follow another green path beyond, with a right of way sign where it starts.

For the longer route, when you emerge on to the green track paralleled by the old 'park pale', instead of following it right-handed, cross straight over. Leading on into Holbury Wood here is a stile on which I sat to eat lunchtime sandwiches. This gave me the chance to watch woodland wildlife including a jay, a foraging squirrel and a roe deer which unexpect-edly appeared on one of the rides, where it paused briefly to look around before moving on into thick cover. A shoot was on near by and I expect the deer had been disturbed by this.

The public footpath follows the leftward of two rides which diverge from

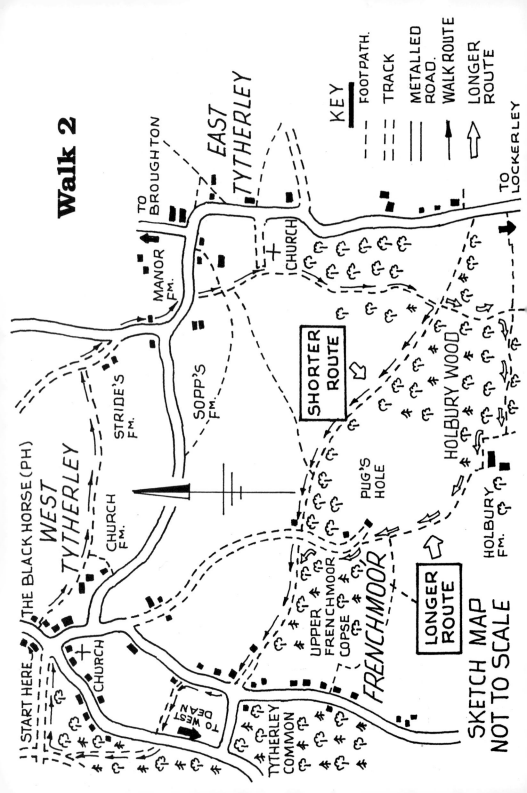

this stile. Oaks and hazels precede a woodland clearing as you head south to the wood's far edge, beyond which a tree-fringed hollow way leads on to join a metalled lane. This is also a public footpath as you follow it right-handed past two pairs of modern cottages followed by an older house. Cypresses, tall pines and other trees flank the lane as it follows a winding course through woodland. As you approach Holbury Farm, which looks south across the Vale of Dean to the hill of the same name, follow where a footpath sign points right-handed. Skirting piggeries to your left, your path bends left by another sign and then soon bends right to cross a plank bridge preceding a double ladder surmounting a high fence.

This protects young trees from damage by deer, which are abundant hereabouts. Your path leads on through the fenced plantation to leave it by means of another double ladder. You then pass through a gate with a waymarking arrow to the left of it. The Pathfinder map shows the footpath now bearing slightly away from the right-hand fence of the field here entered, but I found no visible trace of such a path. You can either follow the field's right-hand margin to its far end and then bear left with it, or make for the right-hand one of three oaks on the ridge just ahead and then keep straight on across arable farmland to descend to a low metal gate through the field boundary below. Cross this to follow the right-hand edge of two pastures, passing through two more gateways, then heading diagonally right across a third pasture with Pug's Hole farmhouse behind you on your right. Joining a metalled driveway, you follow this left-ahead and then right-handed past a cottage and on through woodland, at the far end of which the two alternative middle sections of the walking route reunite.

Here you turn left by a right of way sign to follow a north-westerly continuation of the green track first encountered at the approach to Holbury Wood. Flanked on your left by Upper Frenchmoor Copse, this passes a thatched house on your right before leading out on to a junction of metalled lanes. Turn right here to the first slight right-hand bend of the lane in question where, on the near side of thatched Lucewood Cottage, a half-hidden sign points out a footpath preceded by a stile. The path swings right, round the rear of the cottage, then becomes fenced and heads left to another stile, beyond which you cross a metalled lane. A signposted path winds on ahead through unfenced woodland to join a track opposite farm buildings on the Norman Court estate. Follow this track right-handed to a crossing of ways just short of some cottages. Here you turn right to follow a grass-flanked gravel road back to West Tytherley, nearly half a mile ahead, where you emerge on to a road which you follow left-handed back to your starting point.

Chalkland Tracks and Paths around Grateley

WALK 3
Up to **4 hours**
7 miles
Walk begins page 19

Background to the Walk

A 'great lea', or meadow, south-west of the 13th century Church of St. Leonard is said to have given its name to the once remote chalkland village on which this walk is based. Lying just south of the Roman Portway, linking Old Sarum (Sorviodunum) with Silchester (Calleva Atrebatum), Grateley was the setting for a special council called by King Athelstan in AD 925. Its history is otherwise largely uneventful: typical of a farming settlement on the fringe of Salisbury Plain, which in part it remains although its population now includes a large commuter element. Although the main London-Salisbury railway skirts the village, Grateley station was built a mile from it to please the owners of Grateley House, who did not want it right on their doorstep. A second village has sprung up around the station and is still growing. With its village shop, pub and school, the older Grateley remains a well-rounded and largely self-contained community, and its situation away from main roads helps preserve a good measure of the tranquillity of earlier times.

If picturesque old world dwellings are less in evidence in Grateley than in some other small rural villages, there are no grounds for complaint on this score at Quarley, a mile to the north. Small, sequestered, sleepy and with a wealth of thatch and old timber, Quarley — its name means 'a quarter of the lea' or perhaps 'woodland clearing with a mill or where mill-stones are obtained' —

Maps
*Landranger 1:50,000
Sheet 184
Pathfinder 1:25,000
Sheet SU 24/34
Map Reference of
Start/Finish SU279419*

How to get there
From Southampton and Romsey turn left from the A3057 opposite The Duke's Head at Greatbridge to follow B3084 in the Tidworth direction. After crossing the railway by Grateley station immediately turn right for Grateley village, and when you reach this turn right, left, then right again. The Plough is on the corner of Chapel Lane, on your right. Access by bus from Southampton is via Solent Blue service 47 to Winchester and Hampshire Bus services 30/31 from Winchester to Andover, from which connection is made with Grateley

has what a notice in front calls a 'Saxo-Norman' church. Dedicated to St. Michael, this has an 18th century east window and, most notably, its three bells are hung at ground level, to the rear. Quarley Village Hall, a modern building with all that this implies in terms of appearance, is sensibly located well apart from the fine old cottages at the core of this pleasant community. The erstwhile school is now a private dwelling, and Quarley has lacked a pub since the last one was burnt down in the 1920s. The landowner gave villagers the choice of rebuilding the pub or laying on piped water and they opted for Adam's ale instead of a regular local supply of good British beer!

Dominating the landscape is Quarley Hill, a modest, tree-crowned eminence at one time noted among ornithologists as an assembly point in spring for migrating stone curlews from Africa. Surmounted by Iron Age earthworks, the hill is thought by some to have been the place where King Athelstan held his council well over ten centuries ago. It is privately owned and, regrettably, not accessible to the public.

Walk 3

Distance : 7 miles, with a comfortable walking time of up to 4 hours.

Opposite Grateley's Plough Inn a modern cul-de-sac called Hawthorne Close leads to a fenced footpath around the right-hand edge of a football field. We found this weed-infested and worse. Encroaching thorny vegetation badly needed trimming back to clear the way for pleasant walking. We did just manage to squeeze through at the cost of minor stings and scratches. If matters have not been mended by the time you tackle this walk you might do better to walk back along the road leading to the pub and fork right just short of the school to follow the High Street. Towards the far end of the village Manor Farm

by Amport and District bus service No. 1 on weekdays only. Grateley can be reached by train from Southampton by changing at Salisbury for the Andover and Basingstoke line, the station and village at Grateley being a mile apart.

Pub facilities
The Plough Inn.

As well as a good range of brews and wines of the month selected according to season, this Gibbs Mew house at Grateley, a village local turned popular tavern for customers from near and far, has a seven day restaurant renowned for its fish and seafood specialities. Specially featured when I called were Dorset mussels in a cream and wine sauce with crusty garlic bread at under £4.00. Also billed was a mouth-watering Sunday lunchtime invitation to 'sit back and feast on succulent roast beef, roast potatoes, peas and fresh vegetables with lashings of radish sauce' for a modest investment of £4.95.

Quarley village

Food may be ordered between 1200-1400 and between 1900-2130 (until 2200 on Saturdays and Sundays).

A bar counter overhang of thatch helps reinforce the country character of this pub which has been dispensing hospitality for a century and a half. Four rooms for overnight guests preserve its right to be called an inn. Summer visitors can take their drinks into a rear garden where fruit trees flourish. An overflow area helps ensure that there is plenty of room for parking, and walkers are welcome to use the car park if they are also using the pub. Older children are welcome, especially in the restaurant area, but dogs are not admitted. Pub owners Gibbs Mew, of Salisbury, are one of the few surviving older firms of independent brewers and the full range of their products may be sampled at The Plough.

lies to your left. This is another possible site of that local assemblage presided over by King Athelstan. Just beyond where houses on your right end, a footpath sign beckons you right-handed to the edge of an arable field, across which a notional path leads towards the hedgerow on its far side. Surface signs of such a right of way were absent when we looked for it. The farmer, who happened to be ploughing, said it had not been used for years. In the condition in which we found it this

Quarley church. 'have a close look at the ground level belfry, quite unique in our experience'.

was hardly a cause for surprise. Instead of pushing through growing crops or across ploughed ground, we followed a well-defined headland of untilled ground around the right-hand edge of the field. Turning right with the field boundary and then left, this led us to a stepless stile at the end of the path past the football field that reaches this point from Hawthorne Close.

Turn left here (or keep straight on if you have followed the direct path from The Plough) to follow what I hope will you will find as an unmistakable footpath. This leads towards the left-hand end of a hedge which terminates in mid-field. When you reach this, head for a prominent post in another hedgerow farther on. As you approach this you may, or may not, notice that you are crossing the ancient Portway, where Roman chariots once raced past to the bemusement of watching Britons. Through a gap in the far hedge your path emerges to join Grateley Drove, a tall-hedged track of grass and earth which is nevertheless a byway officially open to all traffic. Follow it right-handed to where, after half-a-mile, it joins a metalled lane.

On the two occasions I walked this way there have been caravans and

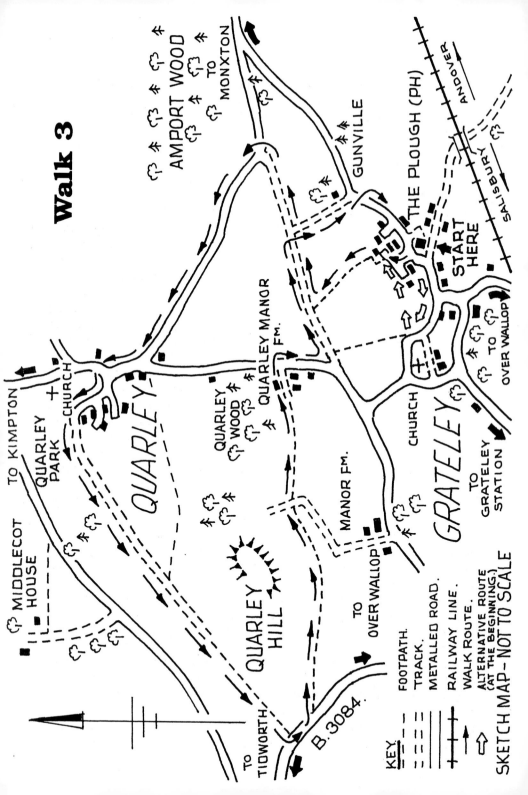

Walk 3

AMPORT WOOD

TO MONXTON

GUNVILLE

THE PLOUGH (PH)

START HERE

TO ANDOVER

TO SALISBURY

TO OVER WALLOP

QUARLEY MANOR FM.

QUARLEY WOOD

QUARLEY MANOR FM.

QUARLEY

CHURCH

QUARLEY PARK

TO KIMPTON

MIDDLECOT HOUSE

QUARLEY HILL

TO OVER WALLOP

MANOR FM.

GRATELEY

CHURCH

TO GRATELEY STATION

TO TIDWORTH

B. 3084.

KEY.

FOOTPATH.

TRACK.

METALLED ROAD.

RAILWAY LINE.

WALK ROUTE.

ALTERNATIVE ROUTE. (AT THE BEGINNING.)

SKETCH MAP — NOT TO SCALE

clapped-out motor coaches serving as dwellings parked illegally at this point, with the added annoyance of snarling dogs on chains to be circumvented. I hope Hampshire County Council will have finally resolved this problem by the time you try this walk — if not, have another go at them! Their officer responsible for dealing with gypsies and other travellers is the man to get in touch with.

Follow the metalled lane left-handed. Across farmland to your right a line of tall trees leads to Amport Wood, while to your left, some two miles distant, looms the pyramidal hump of Quarley Hill, which remains in sight throughout the most of this walk. At the southern end of Quarley your lane joins another, which you follow right-handed. Thatch, flint, a chalk-rubble wall, and a well (I am sure unused now), contribute their individual period charms to a village scene as pleasing as could well be wished for as you approach Quarley war memorial. At the lane junction here turn right, then follow a short-cut path left of the right-hand lane itself. Promptly rejoining the lane, you follow it ahead past Bridge Cottage, an old world idyll we found sadly spoilt by a TV satellite dish propped up against its flower-wreathed well-head. Backed by lovely parkland timber, the little church lies to your left. We found it locked but walked round to its far side to have a close look at the ground level belfry, quite unique in our experience. The bells hang from a frame underneath a protective shingled roof.

Walk back to the war memorial and there bear right to follow what in effect is a blind lane, with yews to the right of it and thatch-and-timber cottages to your left. Soon after rounding a left-hand bend the tarmac road gives way to a gated track of gravel, chalk and grass with, along one stretch, a concreted section. Tall hedged in parts, low hedged or fenced in others, with discarded farm machinery cluttering some sections of grass verge, this farm track-cum-public footpath undulates gently as it follows an almost straight south-westerly course, overlooked by Quarley Hill on one side and by Cholderton Hill on the other. To your right, a mile away, A303 may just be seen, bearing its ceaseless mechanised burden between London and the West.

As a field-edge path your track emerges on to the Tidworth-Romsey road, B3084, which you follow left-handed for a field's length to where a stile on your left precedes a footpath. Follow this uphill along the leftward edge of a pasture, and where the hedge to your left bends left continue ahead to another stile. A yellow arrowhead points your way ahead from here to where a third stile precedes a grass farm track followed by a fourth stile, which you cross. Striking slightly left of where the arrow here points, head for two posts on the ridge ahead. Just left of these cross a stile to follow the right-hand edge of a field with a double-fenced farm track to your right. Angle slightly left of the right-hand fence to cross yet another stile followed

Quarley Hill from the south east of Quarley.

by a horse-jump leading you into a cattle pasture (where we found the cattle friendly!).

Leaving Quarley Hill behind you on your left after passing close to its forbidden upper limits, head diagonally right as directed by the yellow waymarking arrow. This takes you on a converging course with the cattle pasture's left-hand fence, which you follow ahead to a gate and a second pasture. Quarley Wood lies to your left as you continue to a left-hand corner stile at the end of this meadow. Cross this to pass through the grounds of Quarley Manor Farm, which we found littered with all kinds of junk that had nothing at all to do with farming, and so out on to the road beyond. Follow this road right-handed past the lawned grounds of flint-walled Quarley Manor House and a smaller dwelling called The Doll's House. Not many yards ahead the metalled road bends right but you turn left to walk east for a second time along tall-hedged Grateley Drove.

A few hundred yards short of the end of this turn right to follow a tree-hedged bridleway which becomes a gravel track as you pass a thatched cottage on your left. The gravel track leads you out on to a road which you follow right-handed back into Grateley, where The Plough Inn lies to your left as you approach from this direction.

Downland Ways near King's Somborne

WALK 4
Either **4** or **5 hrs**
7 or **9 miles**
Walk begins page 27

Background to the walk

The fragrance of woodsmoke mingled with other agreeable odours of the countryside to make author D. H. Moutray Read think of 'cherry cheeks, pink bonnets and new milk' when he came to King's Somborne seeking material for his *Highways and Byways in Hampshire* when the 20th century was still young. True, the stream beside the village street was no more than 'an open drain', but there were 'colour-washed mud walls', timber-framed dwellings and thatched roofs aplenty to paint the picture of bucolic near-perfection his words convey to those who still read him.

Already, though, there were dwellings of 'staring and uncompromising hideosity' to mar this idyll. All in all, however, the King's Somborne of Edwardian days seems still to have been the unspoilt product of times when country villages were self-contained communities peopled more or less exclusively by those who were born and bred there, earned their living in the neighbourhood and hardly ever journeyed elsewhere except on very special occasions.

A fair measure of the flavour of those times can still be found here. The 'villas' execrated by Moutray Read have become more numerous, but there remains more than a sprinkling of thatch and other delights to preserve the character of an age long before motorists could discover this Test Valley village.

First recorded as 'Swinburnan', which

Maps
Landranger 1:50,000
Sheet 185
Pathfinder 1:25,000
Sheets SU 23/33, SU 42/52 and SU 22/32
Map Reference of
Start/Finish SU362308

How to get there
From Southampton head west to Redbridge roundabout, then follow M271 and A3057 north around Romsey and up the Test Valley to reach King's Somborne about 3 miles short of Stockbridge. Solent Blue bus service 47 between Southampton and Winchester connects with Hampshire Bus service 34 between Winchester and Salisbury via King's Somborne.

Pub Facilities

*Many who seek re-
freshment in appropri-
ate surroundings in an
old world Test Valley
village naturally
gravitate to **The
Crown Inn** on arrival
at King's Somborne.
Records confirm the
grade II listed building
as having existed since
1640, though whether
it has always been a
pub is not so certain. It
certainly has a ghost, a
friendly character
called Fred who patrols
the premises after
closing time.*

*Ringwood Best Bitter
and Boddington's bitter
are both dispensed
here. In cold weather
you can sup your ale
by the warmth of an
open fire. There are no
gaming machines or
jukebox but you can
play darts or the piano
in this pub where
Wurzel Gummidge once
performed for televi-
sion. Children may
come into the lounge
bar or play on swings
and slides in the
garden. Home-made
steak and kidney pie
or other fare may be
ordered on weekdays
or Sundays between
1200-1400 or between
1900-2130 (until 2100
on Sundays) any
evening except Tues-*

placename pundits rather unkindly interpret as
'pig stream', the name Somborne is shared by the
village where this walk starts with two of its
neighbours. King's Somborne, as is self-evident,
was of old a royal property. John of Gaunt, the
fourth son of Edward III, had a palace here and a
deer park, parts of the boundary of which can still
be traced. The Church of St. Peter and St. Paul
preserves some fragments from the early 13th
century but was largely rebuilt in the 1880s. An
inscription on one of the pillars states that the
ring of bells was completed in the year of Queen
Victoria's Jubilee, 1887. Close to the church is the
village school, one of the very first of its kind.
Following its opening in 1842 a prime minister
and other leading lights came along to admire it.
Its construction was inspired by the need, as the
village parson judged it, to raise the morals of
those who lived here — so perhaps the good old
days were not so idyllic after all!

Up Somborne, on the route of the longer version
of this walk, has neither church, school nor pub.
The lack of the latter, although one was promised
by a map that proved out of date, tempted my
walking companion and me to utter the name of
this chalk country hamlet with less than unquali-
fied approval when we arrived there, hot and
thirsty, one rather sweltering summer's day.

Also on the longer route is one of rural Hampshire's best known landmarks, Farley Mount
Monument. Crowning a hill commanding views
across more of the county than can be seen from
almost any other hilltop, this steepled structure
marks the burial place of a horse that saved its
rider's life by leaping into a chalk pit 25 feet deep
while hunting, and surviving to win an important
race at Worthy Down the following year. These
events took place in the 1730s, long before town
and country planning dictated what could be
built, and where! The monument looms near the
western end of Farley Mount Country Park, an

The Crown Inn, Kings Somborne

open space owned by the county council and popular all year round with fresh air seekers from near and far.

Walk 4

Distance: Allow at least 4 hours for the 7-mile route or 5 hours for the 9-mile alternative.

We parked in King Somborne's Old Palace Road, a cul-de-sac to the right of Church Road, which turns right from A3057 directly opposite The Crown Inn as you approach from the Romsey direction. Returning from there to the main road, you pass on your left the triangular village green with its war memorial, adjacent church and the 1842 school. Follow A3057 right-handed for a few yards and there turn right beside the premises of a chair seater and basket maker — an old country craft if ever there was one.

A tile-topped wall of chalk rubble, flint and brick flanks the often dry bourne — the original 'pig stream' — that borders Old Vicarage Lane, which you now follow. Next comes The Old Vicarage itself, followed by a strip of grass and the ford, paralleled by a footbridge, which takes you right-

days. Buffet meals for parties of walkers can be laid on by prior arrangement. The pub is open between 1100-1500 and 1900-2300 on weekdays and at the usual times on Sundays. You can park here if you ask first.

*In King's Somborne's Winchester Road, **The Andover Arms** was recently reopened by new owners Wiltshire Brewery of Tisbury. Three own real ales (Stonehenge, Old Grumble and Old Devil) are complemented by two guest ales, two draught ciders including Old Basic Scrumpy and their own brewed real ginger beer, 'the same strength as Pils'. This is a pub where food looms large — home-cooked ham, omelettes, mixed grills, breaded plaice, moussaka, spaghetti and much else besides, not least a three-course lunch on Sundays which needs to be booked at least two days beforehand. There is also a vegetarian menu and a restaurant area.*

Cottage, King's
Somborne

Original beams and an open fire help to remind you that this, too, is a grade II listed building. Originally three cottages with a drovers' lean-to at the front, it has been restored to earlier status as an authentic village pub, with no pool table or jukebox (though there is a fruit machine). Table skittles are played and there is a darts room. Children are admitted for meals and can also enjoy the sizeable garden. Just across the road from the pub there is space for parking.

handed into Winchester Road. As you follow this left-handed you pass The Andover Arms on your right. Cruck Cottage, on the same side, derives its name from its style of construction, with a massive curved beam as part of the framework of timbers supporting the walls and thatched roof. A little way farther along, on your left, a buttressed barn of thatch and whitewash which serves nowadays as a garage adjoins another, thatched and weatherboarded, which has been transformed into a dwelling. These are excellent examples of the way redundant farm buildings of great visual delight can be adapted for modern use rather than be left to fall into ruin.

A narrow lane from the left joins your road before it curves right to reach a fork where you keep left, uphill, to where a hedge angles right-handed. To the right of this hedge is a signposted footpath. Follow this along the upper edge of a sloping field to a stile, having crossed which your path follows the right-hand edge of another field, with the hedge now to your right. Beyond a second stile, where a notice warns about keeping dogs on leads, your path is fenced on the left and hedged on the right, with a hillslope plantation to your left. Where this ends you cross a farm road and carry on along a farm track-cum-green lane, with a hedge to your right.

You now follow a view-commanding ridge, with Little Somborne backed by woodland on rising ground beyond the dry chalk valley to your left. As you carry on north-east, with a hedge to your right, the field-edge path you now follow heads downhill to a wire fence around which you walk to join a yew-bordered lane, which leads you right-handed. For the shorter walk, keep to this lane, which soon joins another at a T-junction. Here turn left, then after a further few hundred yards take a yew-bordered green lane which turns right.

The alternative approach to this is to follow the first yew-bordered lane right-handed for a few yards, then cross a stile on your left to follow a well-defined path with a hedge at first on your left, then arable farmland on both sides. A hedge reappears on your left as you approach an iron swing-gate preceding a final few footpath yards alongside a terrace of thatch-and-brick cottages. This brings you out on to the lane that climbs south through Up Somborne. A mixture of modern and period dwellings flanks the route that you follow right-handed through this small village, emerging uphill from which you reach a T-junction of lanes where you turn right. Scattered yews plus some hawthorns border the byway you now follow west for just over a quarter of a mile before turning left to join the green lane reached at this point by the shorter route.

Luxuriant wayside herbage is athrong in summer with butterflies as you follow the green lane south along a valley flanked by fields rising east and west to hilltop woodland. Scattered yews add to the charm of this placid section of the walk, which is also popular with riders. A fallen tree across the track obliged a party on horseback to diverge on to neighbouring farmland on the day when we tried this route.

The yew-mantled northern slopes of the hill crowned by Farley Mount loom larger as you approach a junction of byways surrounded by trees at a point where a driveway leads left to Forest of Bere Farm. This latter may seem in the wrong place until one remembers that the ancient royal hunting ground so called once spread much farther across Hampshire than its remnants do today. The forest in its heyday was in two separate parts: Bere Portchester, east of the Meon Valley, and Bere Ashley, west of Winchester, where the forest's name is no longer used but many large woods remain.

A few yards ahead, where the track forks, those who opt for the shorter route should bear right to follow a metalled lane — part of the road first built by the Romans to link Winchester with Old Sarum. Beacon Hill's north-facing slope, covered partly with yews and partly with greensward, rises to your left as you now head west for half a mile to where the metalled road is joined by a track from the left and bends right-handed. Bordered by yews on its right-hand side, a green lane now leads you left-ahead from a sign indicating it as part of The Clarendon Way long distance walk between Winchester and Salisbury.

For the longer route, instead of forking right just past the Forest of Bere

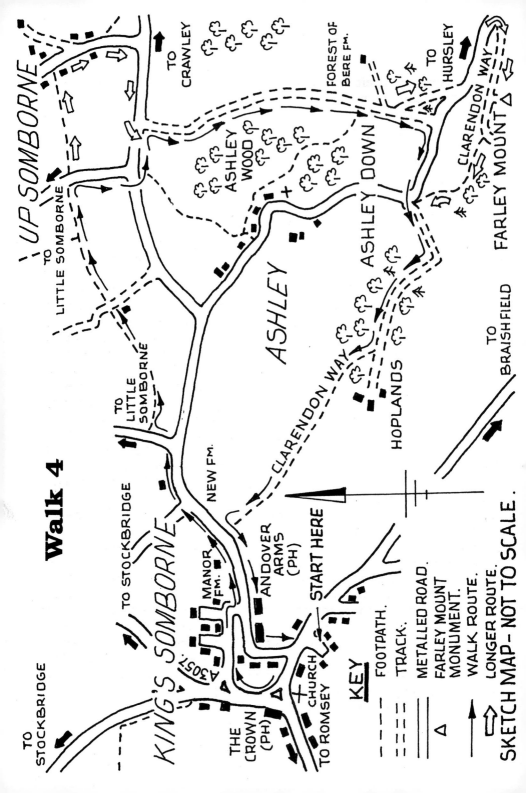

Walk 4

SKETCH MAP – NOT TO SCALE.

KEY

– – –	FOOTPATH.
= = =	TRACK.
———	METALLED ROAD.
△	FARLEY MOUNT MONUMENT.
→	WALK ROUTE.
⇨	LONGER ROUTE.

TO STOCKBRIDGE

UP SOMBORNE

TO LITTLE SOMBORNE

TO CRAWLEY

FOREST OF BERE FM.

TO HURSLEY

CLARENDON WAY

FARLEY MOUNT △

ASHLEY WOOD

ASHLEY DOWN

ASHLEY

CLARENDON WAY

HOPLANDS

TO BRAISHFIELD

KING'S SOMBORNE

TO STOCKBRIDGE

TO LITTLE SOMBORNE

NEW FM.

MANOR FM.

ANDOVER ARMS (PH)

START HERE

THE CROWN (PH)

CHURCH

TO ROMSEY

A3057

Farm turning, keep left-ahead along a track with woodland on both sides. Where this joins the metalled road last mentioned, follow the latter left-handed, uphill below a yewy escarpment, to the entrance to Farley Mount Country Park. Here you turn right to follow a rising gravel track beyond a car park and vehicle barrier which someone had gone to a great deal of trouble to breach when I last saw it. From the crest of the rise an earth track climbs left-handed between fences to the mound topped by Farley Mount Monument, which you can sit inside while reading the inscription explaining its origin.

Resuming your walk, head back down the fenced earth track and then turn left to follow a grass path along the rim of Beacon Hill. Where this path soon forks, bear right, then within a fairly short distance veer back left-handed to rejoin the ridge path, which you follow to where a wood starts. Here bear right by a Clarendon Way sign to follow a bridleway steeply downhill with beech and yew woodland to your left and a field to your right. Where the gradient slackens your scenic path follows a fenced course across a field. It crosses the next field without benefit of fences to reach the metalled road heading north-west from Farley Mount Country Park to King's Somborne.

Instead of joining this, turn left to follow the green lane with yews on its right-hand side which the shorter route also follows, the two routes having now reunited. Woodland rims the steep grassy incline ahead as you approach a metalled gate through which you turn right to follow a track diagonally uphill through a yew grove. Climbing out of this, your track bends left to coincide once more with the Roman road already mentioned. Trees on your left line the earth track you now follow. When you reach a track junction where the right fork carries a 'private — no access' notice, take a path signposted as part of The Clarendon Way which heads half-right from the cleft of the fork.

This leads through a small wood to a stile. Cross this to follow the right-hand edge of a field, with a wood, then a thick hedge, and then a fence to the right of the footpath. After crossing two double stiles between individual paddocks, you negotiate a third double stile preceding an incline in country so quiet you could be miles from anywhere. A green lane then leads you over a ridge to reveal King's Somborne, just ahead. Village lights twinkled a welcome when my walking companion and I breasted this rise in the winter dusk. The green track leads on down to the road which you follow left-handed back into the village. For Old Palace Road, if you left your car there, keep straight on to a T-junction with Church Road, which you briefly follow left-handed and then turn right to regain your transport.

River Valley and Downland near Fullerton

WALK 5
Up to **4** or **5 hours**
For **8** or **10 miles**
Walk begins page 35

Background to the walk

Until much of the route of the former 'Sprat and Winkle' railway between Romsey and Andover was taken over by Hampshire County Council and suitably surfaced for use by walkers, the Test Valley's middle reaches were not well supplied with public footpaths. Matters were improved by the creation of The Test Way long distance walk, which snakes north for 44 miles from Totton to Inkpen Beacon, in Berkshire. The start of this route follows two sample miles of this walk.

The River Test being generally acknowledged as the world's most famous trout stream, fishing rights are a major source of income to estates along its banks. Well maintained paths provided for their guests by riparian owners are carefully bracketed by signs restricting use of them to fishermen. The waterways served by these paths wind their multi-channelled courses between cattle pastures, reedy recesses and groves of willows overlooked by the Hampshire chalk which gives birth to the river not many miles upstream and which is the other prime contributor to the scenery of this walk.

There is no village at the point where the walk starts. Fullerton, half a mile away, consists of a manor house, a farm, a handful of cottages and a one-time water-mill which has been converted, like so many, into a luxury private dwelling. For all its relative insignificance, Fullerton, whose name derives from the Old English for 'farmstead or

Map
Landranger 1:50,000
Sheet 185
Pathfinder 1:25,000
Sheet SU 23/33
Map Reference of
Start/Finish SU382390

How to get there
From Southampton
follow A36, M271 and
A3057 north around
Romsey and along the
Test Valley. At
Stockbridge briefly
follow A30 eastward
before resuming
A3057, along which, a
mile beyond Leckford,
you bridge the Test
and then immediately
turn left into the car
park for The Mayfly.
Solent Bus service 47
between Southampton
and Winchester con-
nects with Hampshire
Bus service 32 be-
tween Winchester and
Salisbury via
Stockbridge and
Longstock, which
passes The Mayfly.
Hampshire Bus service
901 between Romsey,

The Mayfly

Stockbridge and Winchester via Danebury and Farley Mount passes through Longstock on summer season Sundays only, Romsey being accessible from Southampton on Sundays by Southampton Citybus service 7, and by rail.

Pub facilities
The Mayfly was once the home of a small-holder who reared pigs and other livestock. As a licensed establishment it used to be called the Seven Stars, the present name being chosen as more appropriate to a location where the mayfly imitation has been cast by generations of trout fishermen. An unpretentious exterior belies a beamy bar with all the trimmings of a traditional, old world hostelry. The pub was once owned by Weyhill Brewery, a local concern taken over long ago by Strong & Co. of Romsey, absorbed in their turn by Whitbread. Open from 1100-2300 on weekdays and at the usual times on Sundays, a prime feature of The

village of the fowlers or bird-catchers', once had a railway station at a point where the line from Andover was joined by another which ran to Hurstbourne on the Andover—London line. This latter was one of those railways built for no very obvious reason in a fit of Victorian exuberance and doomed to economic failure almost from the moment when it opened. Passenger trains, which quite often carried no passengers at all, last traversed it in 1931, whilst the Romsey—Andover line, much of it built on the course of an earlier canal, survived until the mid-1960s.

The wholly delightful village of Leckford, a mile downstream from The Mayfly and with a name which means 'a ford at or over a leat or channel', has many thatched cottages 300 years old or more. Once the homes of farm workers, river keepers and others locally employed in traditional rural occupations, they are now lived in by retired or active staff members of the John Lewis Partnership, a trust founded for the benefit of employees by store owner John Spedan Lewis when he disposed of his personal interest. In 1928 he bought Leckford Abbas estate, added to it by subsequent purchases and turned over the whole of it to the trust named after him. The 4,000 acre

Mayfly is its riverside garden. When the weather is cold or wet you can still look out on to the river from the comfort of a conservatory leading off from the main bar area.

Smoked River Test trout and a choice of 40 or more different cheeses are special to The Mayfly, and you can order food between 1200-1400 and 1900-2100 daily. Meals are at bar prices, and the pub is recommended in Egon Ronay's 'Good Food in Pubs and Inns'. The usual range of Whitbread brews are on tap. There is an area for children. Pub-using walkers are welcome to use the pub car park, there being no other convenient place in the immediate neighbourhood for parking. Customers travel here from long distances, often using this riverside hostelry as a halfway point to meet friends from far away places.

Fresh wild salmon features on traditional English menus at **The Peat Spade** *in Longstock. This is another pub to which people home in from a distance, it being in no sense a 'village local'*

property extends to the village of Longstock and includes fishing rights on the Test which are enjoyed by Partnership members, all employees of the Partnership, past or present, being called 'partners'.

Longstock, on the other side of the Test, is long indeed — a picturesque village strung out along a lane which meanders north in the general direction of Andover from just west of Stockbridge. The second syllable of Longstock's name has been claimed to derive from the one-time presence of stakes, piles or a timber bridge, or perhaps a combination of all these, unless it means 'outlying farm or hamlet', as another authority suggests. Thatch and half-timbering abound in what was once a self-contained, well-knit and busy community of country people pursuing a range of occupations linked with the soil or with maintaining the very fabric of village life. Latter-day Longstock is mainly a place to which people retire or from which they commute to urban employment, returning home each evening or at weekends to what is little more than a parody of country life as it once was. A century ago it boasted a racecourse patronised by Edward VII the then Prince of Wales. Actress Lillie Langtry often stayed in the neighbourhood when the royal racing enthusiast was also in residence.

Not quite three miles to the west looms Danebury Ring, one of southern England's most notable Iron Age hill forts. Excavations in recent years have revealed much about local life between 600BC and AD50, when Danebury — a corruption of 'Dunbury' meaning 'fortified place' — was home to cultivators and herdsmen who lived in thatched round huts within a formidable ring of earthworks. Moving all that earth about must have been thirsty work indeed. Not only were there no pubs but also, presumably, then as now, no surface water on the dry downs, and one cannot help wondering how those pre-Roman hut-dwellers

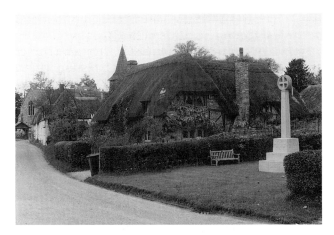

Longstock village

despite its village centre location. Built around 1870 as a pub and brewery combined, it was sold off by Gale's of Horndean fairly recently and is now a free house. It has a small dining room and a large garden. Weekday opening times in summer are 1100-1500 and 1800-2300 and in winter 1200-1500 and 1900-2300, Sunday opening times being as usual. Food may be ordered between 1200-1400 and 1900-2130. Well-behaved dogs are allowed but there are no special facilities for children. Walkers who opt to start here may use the pub car park if they first ask permission.

organised their liquid essentials, especially in times of siege by those against whom they constructed these very elaborate defences. Now owned by Hampshire County Council, the site is open to the public, and at Andover an Iron Age Museum exhibits local finds.

Walk 5

Distance: Allow 5 hours for the 10-mile walk, or 4 hrs. for the 8-mile route, omitting Danebury Ring.

Leaving The Mayfly car park, turn right to follow the main road over the river bridge and the adjacent former railway bridge, then turn left to join The Test Way long distance walk at its halfway point ('Totton 22m, Inkpen Beacon 22m'). A path by a brick wall leads to the skew double arch of brick that you just walked over and through which you now pass to follow a narrow and twisty gravel path flanked by trees and bushes along the old railway's course. With the A3057 to your left you now head south for two miles along a route punctuated every so often by iron bridges still bearing traces of soot from the smoke of steam railway engines which last passed this way in the mid-60s, at one point by a wayside seat and a pair of huts once used by railwaymen, and along another short stretch with glimpses of old cottages at Leckford. To your right the river is mostly invisible in a broad, flat, willowy wilderness running parallel with your path.

Beyond the fifth overbridge, which has had to be strengthened with metal struts since railway days, carry on for a few yards before turning right to follow a path signposted 'To Longstock'. This leads back along the rim of the old railway cutting to the bridge just passed under, alongside which you join and follow left-handed Bunny Lane. The name of his byway apparently has to do with the culverts and bridges, called 'bunnies', by which it crosses successive arms of the River Test. Thatched fishing huts and 'private' signs remind the passer-by that this is all part of that Leckford Estate over which John Lewis 'Partners' reserve the right to cast a silken line in pursuit of wild trout.

The last river crossing precedes Longstock, with The Peat Spade pub to your right as you emerge on to a road flanked by as varied an assortment of thatch and half-timbering as might be hoped would gladden the eye in a river valley village where both abound. Directly opposite Bunny Lane's end is a war memorial in a miniature village green, with seats around it ideal for a contemplative interlude while you gather breath for what lies ahead.

Head south now for a few yards before turning right to follow Church Lane, with steepled St. Mary's Church to your left. There has been a church here for hundreds of years but the present structure bears all the hallmarks of Victorian handiwork. Approaching via the 1907 lych gate, I found the church locked, but read at the door a verse which hints at unseen treasures within: 'Enter this door / as if the floor / within were gold / and every wall / of jewels, all / of wealth untold / as if a choir / in robes of fire / were singing here / nor shout, nor rush, but hush / for God is here'.

Rejoining Church Lane, follow it uphill to where its metalled surface soon ends. Continue along a lesser gradient for a mile to where, at the summit point of this hard-surfaced, unmetalled byway, you pass some brick barns on your left. Wide views over gently undulating agricultural chalkland spread away to your left here. Carry on, now, along a grassy, hedged descent from which right-hand views stretch as far as Beacon Hill, in far north Hampshire. A small left-hand wood of ash and sycamore precedes your emergence on to a junction of metalled roads at Danebury Down. Here I could not resist the temptation to extend what I had meant to be a mere eight-miler to a marathon 10-mile tramp by carrying on to Danebury Ring, the Iron Age hill fort now tantalisingly near. **If you choose to omit this, take the right-forking road, signposted to Redrice and Andover.** Otherwise, having turned right at the end of Church Lane, fork left to take the road signposted to Danebury Ring and Grateley.

A few hundred yards downhill along this, turn left through a gate alongside a cattlegrid to follow the paved road that nowadays leads to

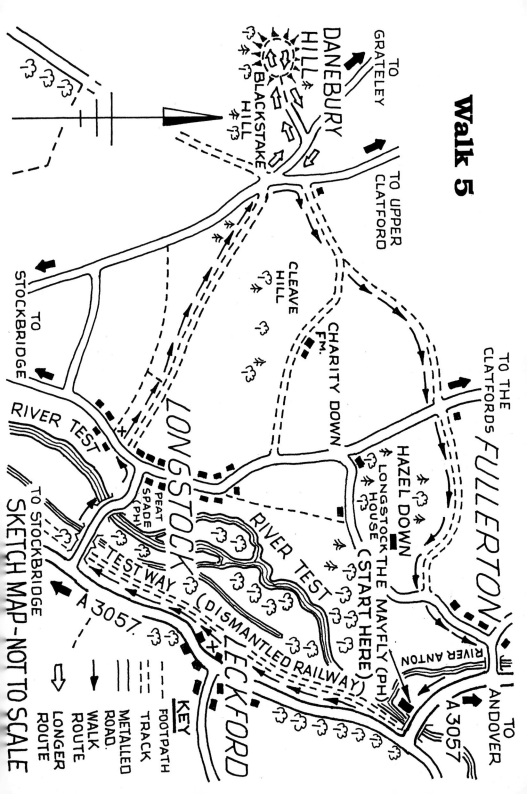

Walk 5

TO GRATELEY

TO UPPER CLATFORD

DANEBURY HILL

BLACKSTAKE HILL

TO STOCKBRIDGE

CLEAVE HILL

CHARITY DOWN

CHARITY FM.

TO THE CLATFORDS

FULLERTON

HAZEL DOWN

LONGSTOCK HOUSE

LONGSTOCK THE MAYFLY (PH) (START HERE)

RIVER TEST

PEAT SPADE (PH)

LONGSTOCK

RIVER TEST

RIVER ANTON

TO ANDOVER

A 3057

TEST WAY

(DISMANTLED RAILWAY)

LECKFORD

TO STOCKBRIDGE

A 3057.

SKETCH MAP - NOT TO SCALE

KEY
— FOOTPATH
--- TRACK
|| METALLED ROAD.
↓↓ WALK ROUTE
⇑ LONGER ROUTE

Danebury Ring. Notices warn dog-walkers that sheep are grazed within the confines of this area to help keep the downland turf in good order. From where the paved road ends, at the car park, a well-defined uphill path leads on to a concrete pillar marking one of the Ordnance Survey's triangulation stations. A boarded walkway then leads through the outer earthwork of the prehistoric fort to where a leftward path mounts the much higher inner earthwork. Make your way clockwise around the rim of this truly prodigious monument to prehistoric achievement, which must surely have been the fruit of a massive slave-labour operation. The sheer muscle-power that was involved in building the fort is almost beyond imagining.

Beeches break the force of westerly winds sweeping over these heights and, for the most part, these trees fortunately withstood the destructive gales of '87 and '90. Pleasingly dotted about the greensward outside the inner and outer earthworks of the fort are junipers, a chalkland shrub banished from many areas by intensive farming.

Never far from sight or sound here is Middle Wallop Airfield, from which helicopter pilots were audibly undergoing training as I circuited Danebury Ring. Back at the East Gate, where I had entered, I took a flinty leftward track as an alternative way back from the earthworks themselves to the public road, which I followed right-handed back to the fork at Danebury Down. Turn sharp left here to **rejoin the eight-mile route** and head downhill to a right-hand gateway by some tall pines. At this point turn right to follow a fenced gravel byway gently downhill between arable fields. Where the gravelled way fairly soon forks right, keep left-ahead along a fenced grass-and-earth 'bridleway' (so-called on a sign at this point, although strictly speaking it is a byway theoretically open to all traffic). This track curves gently to the right as it follows the floor of a streamless valley, with bordering fences spreading out to embrace a belt of scrub and greensward as you approach the Longstock-Goodworth Clatford road.

Cross this, disregard a well-defined track which leads left-ahead, and keep to a grassy valley track flanked by fences. Overlooked from the right by the scrub-speckled slopes of Hazel Down, where remnants of a prehistoric field system can still be detected and Longstock House peeps out between hilltop trees, your downhill track becomes bush-bordered. As a hedged grass-and-gravel byway it brings you out on to a lane which you follow left-handed to Fullerton. Cottages on your left precede an old chalk-rubble wall shielded from the weather by thatch-and-tile coping, while on your right a brick-and-flint barn directly faces Fullerton Manor Farm. At a lane junction here turn right to cross the Test just north of Fullerton Mill House and join the busy A3057. Watch out for speeding traffic as you follow this right-handed for a few hundred yards back to The Mayfly.

A Field and Forest Walk from Wherwell

WALK 6
Up to **5 hours**
8 miles
Walk begins page 41

Background to the Walk

Wherwell, pronounced 'Whirrell' or even 'Wurrell' but never as spelt, except by strangers, is thought to derive from the Old English for 'spring provided with a kettle or cauldron'. Just why such devices should ever complement a spring is not explained by the experts on the origin of placenames, some of whom, in any case, offer other explanations. One such suggestion would have us believe that the name ought to have an 'o' instead of an 'e' in the first syllable, by way of reminding posterity of the character of a lady who founded a nunnery here in Saxon times.

The lady concerned was Elfrida, the widow of King Edgar, who murdered her late husband's son to divert the succession to her own offspring, and became an abbess allegedly to salve her conscience about this and other transgressions. Edgar himself was no saint. Before meeting Elfrida he sent a courtier, Earl Ethelwold, to check out her wifely potentialities. Elfrida exerted her feminine wiles to such effect that Ethelwold, desiring her for himself, sent an unfavourable report to his royal master. When the King found he had been tricked he invited Ethelwold out hunting in Harewood Forest, and promptly slew him instead of a deer. A monument, Deadman's Plack, was later erected where this may have happened.

Quarrelsome nuns and other problems beset later abbesses at Wherwell. Episcopal intervention sought to restore monastic discipline to what had

Maps
Landranger 1:50,000 Sheet 185
Pathfinder 1:25,000 Sheets SU 24/34, SU 44/54, SU 23/33 & SU 43/53
Map Reference of Start/Finish
SU389409

How to get there
From Southampton follow westbound A3024, M271 and then A3057 up the Test Valley around Romsey and Stockbridge. After crossing the Test by The Mayfly pub, just past the Chilbolton turn-off, take the first turning right from A3057 for Wherwell. Bus access from Southampton is by Solent Blue service 47 to Winchester, Hampshire Bus service 32 from Winchester to Stockbridge and Hampshire Bus service 99 from Stockbridge to Andover, passing through Wherwell.

Pub facilities
The White Lion
Traditional Sunday lunch with a choice of two roasts including beef is served at this Whitbread pub in Wherwell, which attracts many customers from Andover and farther afield. Meals are served every lunchtime and evening except Sunday evening. Three real ales and bed and breakfast accommodation are available and children are admitted to the lower bar area. Walkers who ask first may leave their cars in the pub car park.

The White Lion is open from 1000-1430 (until 1500 on Saturdays) and from 1900-2300 on Mondays and Tuesdays (1800-2300 from Wednesdays to Saturdays), and at the usual hours on Sundays, the pub takes orders for meals between 1200-1400 and in the evenings until 2130 except Sundays, when no food is served. Local mushrooms and trout are among specialities. Bar food ranges from sandwiches and salads to chillies, curries, and meat and vegetable pasties, to

become a disorderly house, one measure to this end being a ban by Bishop William of Wykeham on overnight male visitors! Following the Dissolution the nunnery was demolished and the house called Wherwell Priory, close to the church, rose in its stead as the family seat of subsequent owners of Wherwell Estate. The present Church of St. Peter and Holy Cross was built in the 1850s to replace a much more modest predecessor which, judging from pictures of it inside today's church, had little to commend it from an architectural standpoint. This was in contrast with the cottages of many who lived in Wherwell, far-famed as these still are, with their thatch, exterior plaster and half-timbering in a range of agreeably eyecatching permutations, as the very epitome of old England at its picture-postcard best.

Chilbolton too is picturesque, though with not quite the exquisite quality of 'olde worlde' perfection that makes sightseers reach for their cameras at Wherwell. The name apparently confirms original ownership by a character called Ceolbeald and was first recorded in 909 as 'Ceolboldingtun'. Its Church of St. Mary did not escape Victorian restoration but still preserves much from earlier days, notably a 13th century chancel. The tower is 19th century. Chilbolton's chief claim to historical fame perhaps dates from more recent times when, in 1944, American glider-borne troops were despatched from a nearby airfield to assist beleaguered comrades at the 'Battle of the Bulge'.

Chilbolton and Wherwell lie on opposite banks of the Test and are linked with each other by a footpath which bridges the river at three points. You will follow it on this walk, as you also will the ancient track between Wherwell and the forest which played a significant part in its history thanks to a certain murderous monarch, the perfidy of a certain courtier and the efforts towards atonement of a lady known to both. Although once a royal hunting ground, Harewood

mention typical items. A traditional Sunday lunch includes a choice of beef and one other roast and there is a substantial evening menu. Children are welcome in the family area and three rooms are available for bed and breakfast accommodation.

An open fire, exposed beams and period items such as a warming pan and a display of old fowling pieces go with a pub which traces its history back to the early 1600s and which once flourished as a coaching inn. Local tradition has it that during the English Civil War shots fired by Cromwell's cannon at Wherwell Priory fell short, one striking the front door of The White Lion and another falling down the chimney.

Forest has been in private ownership for many centuries. It is still quite big enough and wild enough to deserve to be called a forest, with wildlife to match, including two kinds of deer, though you will be lucky to see either on this walk — especially at midday and with talkative companions!

The White Lion pub at Wherwell is within yards of the old station, now hard to recognise as such and buried away among houses built since the line was closed in 1956. The railway concerned ran from Hurstbourne to Fullerton and was built as a double line, albeit that traffic was sparse from the time it was opened, in 1885. In 1913 the line was singled. Passenger trains ceased to run in 1931, but World War II briefly gave the line to Longparish new purpose by way of a bomb storage depot in Harewood Forest. Parts of the network of concrete roads which served the depot are visible signs of the forest's wartime function.

Walk 6

Distance : Allow up to 5 hours for this 8-mile walk.

From The White Lion Hotel cross the road that leads to Fullerton and follow a downhill lane directly opposite the pub. Beyond a few cottages and

Wherwell, 'Tall trees rise just behind these cottages to provide the perfect setting to round off their quite outstanding old world delight'

outbuildings you cross one of the arms of the River Test before following a signposted leftward path to the Church of St. Peter and the Holy Cross. It stands in a green and quiet corner between the village and Wherwell Priory, the grounds of which are directly adjoining. The present mansion is white, with a Tuscan porch and a cupola, and dates from the early 19th century.

Carry on past the church to recross the Test and follow Church Street between some of the many lovely old thatched and timber-framed cottages which are such a feature of Wherwell. The most photographed of these dwellings are those that lie to your right as you emerge on to B3420 and follow it right-handed. Tall trees rise just behind these cottages to provide the perfect setting to round off their quite outstanding old world delight.

Opposite Priory Cottage turn left to follow an unmetalled byway between the surviving brick piers of a demolished railway arch. Beyond this a footpath joins the track from your left. Carry on ahead, past a gate, to follow a rising, tree-shaded hollow lane between gently undulating fields. As signs indicate, you are now on part of The Test Way long distance walk which runs from the mouth of the river at Totton to Inkpen Beacon in Berkshire, and which leaves the Test at Longparish, a few miles north-east of Wherwell.

Your hollow lane, a mere track such as the packmen of bygone centuries used to convey their merchandise from village to village, presently dips to pass farm outbuildings and a bungalow called New Barn. A Test Way sign here keeps you on course as your track bears slightly right-handed to climb between more trees, and then with trees on your right-hand side only, to cross a small ridge. From the top of the rise Harewood Forest comes into view, spreading its broad, almost wholly deciduous mass before you beyond the farmland that still lies ahead. The view to your right from here takes in a cross-section of the Test Valley, with north Hampshire's agricultural chalkland presenting yet more of itself beyond.

Your track, here a green lane, reaches and follows the forest edge in a right-hand direction. At a track junction where the forest border soon bends right, you turn right to reach a scattering of outbuildings called Park Farm. As a sign here indicates, the Test Way now turns left to take you into the forest itself, where in a valley you take two successive right-hand turns. By the second one I sat with my back against a tree to eat lunch and to watch the treetop antics of a grey squirrel. A foraging party of long-tailed tits swung acrobatically from twig-ends in an oak just in front of me before passing on to seek fresh food supplies in other treetops. Wildlife interludes like these enhance the pleasure on any walk.

A track on which wartime concrete shows through in places as a reminder of Harewood Forest's role as a bomb dump, skirts a grassy right-hand slope before probing on through oaks and conifers. Soon you pass a row of sheds used for the mass-rearing of chickens by one of England's leading producers. Farther on is a piggery and then yet more chicken sheds as you head towards where what is now a well-defined road swings right to pass under an old brick railway arch.

This brings you out on to the Wherwell-Longparish road, B3048, which you follow left-handed, uphill, then turn right to follow a tree-lined track signposted as a public footpath. A few hundred yards ahead, by a house and farm buildings called Gavelacre, you join and follow left-handed a macadamised driveway which leads out on to the A303 dual carriageway. Follow the highway verge right-handed, crossing two branches of the Test before turning right to follow a lane signposted to Bransbury.

Within a quarter of a mile you reach the hamlet of this name, which has a satisfying proportion of old thatched cottages among its mere handful of dwellings. Here you disregard two successive turnings left and cross a substantial tree-fringed waterway which, until lately, seems not to have been thought worthy of being called 'river' or, indeed, of being named on maps at all despite being one of the Test's major tributaries. By common consent this has changed, and we may call it the River Dever, as the Ordnance Survey now acknowledges.

After crossing the Dever follow a track right-handed to where a sign indicates a bushed-in left-turning tributary track as a byway theoretically open to all traffic. The way ahead, which you follow, is a mere bridleway, hedged on your left in its early stages and with scrub woodland to your right. This continues as a green lane and then as a track just inside the wood, at the far end of which a gate marks your point of emergence on to grassy Bransbury Common, a grazing area bracketing where the Dever joins the Test. Your path, not well-defined now, follows the leftward edge

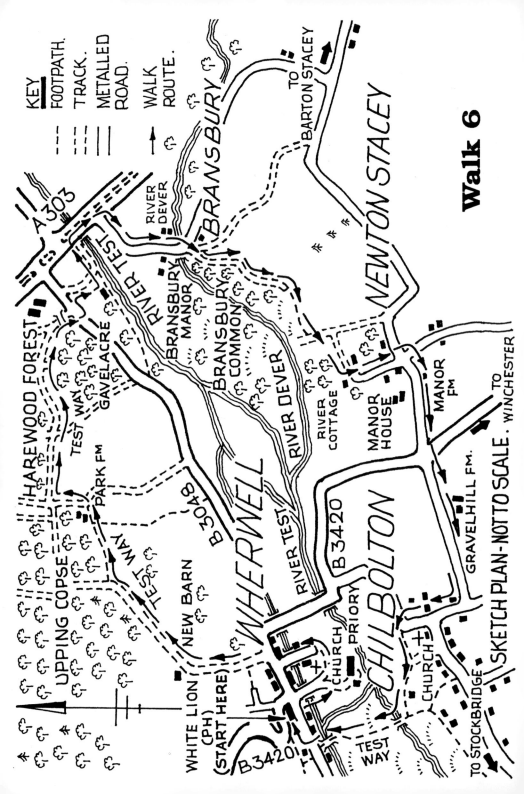

Walk 6

of the common, with a hedgerow to your left, leading to a gate flanked by a stile. The gate when I reached it bore a notice reading 'Private, no public right of way'. Someone before me, noting this not to be in accord with the facts, had therefore scored through the first two words — all credit to the person concerned, whoever they may be! On the stile's far side, when I crossed it, I found another sign, saying 'Footpath', pointing the way to the route just followed.

Anyway, cross this stile to follow a hedged green lane. Within a very short distance another green lane leads you right-handed to Newton Stacey, which begins with prettily sited River Cottage. From here the lane becomes metalled and soon bends left to a lane junction where you turn right. Newton Stacey's few dwellings pass behind as you now head west for half a mile to reach the Winchester-Wherwell road, B3420. Cross this and carry on along another lane for three-quarters of a mile to reach Chilbolton where, as you enter the village, your lane is joined by another and bends right.

Picturesque cottages flank the road you now follow north-west. Disregard the road that turns left through the village centre and pass the Church of St. Mary on your left as you carry on to a bend where you cross a stile by a gate on your left. You now follow a well-trodden path across river valley meadowland. With the village now to your left, you keep right-handed of a hedge which flanks the pasture on that side to reach a swing-gate beside the river. Pass through this to join another path which leads you right-handed by way of a metal footbridge over one of the arms of the Test. You are now on Chilbolton Common where, the very first time I came this way, cattle belly-deep in water combined with the spreading riverine pasture to provide an idyllic scene.

Your path leads across the grassy common to a wooden footbridge over another arm of the Test. A short macadamised section of path precedes a much longer wooden footbridge spanning the junction of two more branches of this multi-channelled trout stream. A few yards farther on the now handrailed path joins the road to Fullerton. Follow this to the left, past a right-hand cottage, and then turn right to follow a hedged path which, like the path across Chilbolton Common, is part of The Test Way walk.

This path is stepped to cross the old Fullerton-Hurstbourne railway, beyond which you cross a stile to follow the right-hand edge of a rising, chalky field, with a hedge to your right. From the field's far end two hedges flank a metalled few yards of footpath, joining the Andover-Wherwell road where it twists sharply down into the valley. Follow this road right-handed to recross the one-time railway and arrive back at The White Lion Hotel, a few yards beyond.

Exploring Chalk Country around Sparsholt

WALK 7
Up to **4 hours**
6·5 miles.
Walk begins page 48

Background to the Walk

A disappointing feature of Sparsholt is the rarity of thatched dwellings in a chalkland village where one might expect to find many more. Until late in the 19th century Sparsholt's hilltop location created difficulties in ensuring supplies of fresh water for domestic consumption. Wells often ran dry. Even the main one, almost 250 ft. deep and operated by a treadwheel which took 20 minutes to deliver the precious fluid to surface level, could not always be relied upon. Thatched roofs are sadly vulnerable to fire, and many of those that previously graced Sparsholt went up in flames when readily accessible water to dowse such fires was unavailable in the village.

The first step towards remedying this was the installation of a wellhouse as a practical means of celebrating Queen Victoria's Diamond Jubilee. This did away with the need for a treadwheel but did not make water any more plentiful. Eleven more years were to pass before a local benefactor, Samuel Bostock, arranged for piped water to serve the village while also having it laid on at his own place of residence, Lainston House, east of Sparsholt.

One hears a lot about Lainston in Sparsholt. The mansion in question, now a country house hotel, figured in a tale of love gone wrong involving a lady called Elizabeth Chudleigh. In the year 1744 the lovely Elizabeth stayed as a guest at Lainston House with an aunt as chaperone. One

Maps
Landranger 1:50,000
Sheet 185
Pathfinder 1:25,000
Sheets SU 43/53 and
SU 42/52
Map Reference of
Start/Finish SU438313

How to get there
From Southampton head north via A33 and the old main road to Chandler's Ford, where you turn left just over the railway bridge to follow B3043. Where this joins A31 turn right, then within a few hundred yards keep left-ahead to follow A3090 through Hursley. A mile farther on, at Standon, take the second of two left-hand turnings and at the next lane junction keep right. When you reach Sparsholt after a further two miles keep right, by the church, and right again at the next lane junction to reach The Plough Inn, on your left. Bus

access is via Solent Blue service 47 between Southampton and Winchester and Hampshire Bus or Gemini Travel services 32/34 between Winchester and Sparsholt.

Pub facilities The Plough Inn.
Walkers may use the pub car park but must ask first, for security reasons.

Except in winter, when evening opening is not until 1900 except on Saturdays (1830), The Plough Inn, Sparsholt's only pub, is open from 1100-1500 and from 1830 (1800 Fridays and Saturdays) until 2300 on weekdays, and at the usual times on Sundays. Apart from Mondays and Sunday evenings, plus Tuesday evenings in winter, when food is not served, meals may be ordered between 1200-1400 and between 1830-2100.

The Plough is a village pub first and foremost, but its food is famed afar — everything from 'ploughman's' to specials of the day like beef and ale pie. Italian cuisine, curries and vegetarian

The Plough Inn, Sparsholt

day at the races she caught the eye of a fellow race-goer, the Hon. Augustus Hervey, a gentleman of fashion who seized his chance and became her suitor. She already had a lover, the Duke of Hamilton, whose letters were being intercepted by her disapproving aunt. Miffed at the duke's seeming silence, Elizabeth married Hervey secretly, in the private chapel at Lainston. Years passed before, on a curious whim, she decided to register the marriage, which had by this time already failed. In the meantime she had married a duke — not of Hamilton, but of Kingston. The result, her trial for bigamy, might never have happened but for the tardy registration of her nuptials to Hervey.

Had this marriage taken place at Sparsholt's Church of St. Stephen, the bridal pair would have entered a building not widely different from the one we see today — but which my walking companion and I found to be locked, and so could not visit: a sad comment on the increasing prevalence of organised thievery. Parts of it date from around 1200. The oaken south doorway is surmounted by an inscription recording the year of its installation, 1631, and the names of two churchwardens, but the tower was one of the fruits of 19th century restoration.

The name 'Sparsholt' has a woody sound about it: hardly surprisingly, when one recalls its bygone location on the fringe of the royal Forest of West Bere — and there are still large woods in the neighbourhood, some of which are explored on this walk. Sparsholt perhaps means 'wood of the spear', or where spear-traps were set for wild animals, or which produced the shafts for spears. Again, the 'Spar' part of the name could simply refer to a spar or rafter, or so the placename experts advise. The hamlet of Dean, also on this route, is one of two so-named in Hampshire and simply means 'a place in a valley'. Woods and vales apart, Sparsholt and the countryside immediately around are linked in the public mind with one aspect of rural life above all others — instruction of the young in the skills of modern agriculture. Sparsholt College is attended by students of farming not only from Hampshire but from all over Britain and from around the world.

Walk 7

Distance : Allow 4 hours for this six-and-a-half-mile walk.

From The Plough Inn head back for a few yards towards Sparsholt village centre and then turn right. Disregard Home Lane, which then turns left, and for a very short distance follow the narrow lane which winds north before turning left to follow a driveway-cum-track signposted to Watley Farm. Beyond where you pass between the farmhouse and its outbuildings the driveway soon turns right but you follow a gravel track ahead. This becomes a tree-lined path, crossed by another path which you ignore. Carry on along what again becomes a driveway to the far end of a horse paddock on your left, where you turn left by a footpath sign to follow a fenced grass path at the

dishes all appear on menus, not to mention such favourites as chilli, plus pheasant and rabbit in season. Sunday lunches are regularly served to 80 or 90 people, with a menu including rack of lamb, curries and half chicken. Family parties are well catered for, and there is a special menu for children. The choice of liquid refreshment is lavish, with four real ales (Farmers' Glory, IPA, 6X and Bass), three draught lagers, draught Guinness and cider, and one keg bitter. There are two bars, with a modern, open fireplace giving added warmth and comfort throughout the winter. Five acres of adjoining land include a beer garden, a children's play area and a donkey paddock.

Recent refurbishment of The Plough Inn's living quarters uncovered two ancient fireplaces — an inglenook from the 19th century and another fireplace reckoned to be at least 390 years old. The pub was originally a farmhouse and it has its own resident ghost, a 'grey

Sparsholt Church tower

lady' who seldom shows herself but whose distinctive, cloying perfume is a frequent reminder of her presence. She is also thought to be responsible for a startling occurrence recently on a particularly warm August night, when papers suddenly started flapping and the room where the family were gathered became inexplicably cold, to the great consternation of those present.

rear of right-hand gardens.

This brings you to the western end of Home Lane, which again you ignore and cross to follow the road leading left-ahead past thatched Vaine's Cottage — one of the prettiest in Sparsholt — to the church.

Pause for a moment to admire the handiwork of those who must recently have refurbished the flint-and-brick wall in front of the churchyard before passing through the latter for a close look at the presumably locked church, with its fine oak door from the 17th century.

Leaving the churchyard, cross the road into the car park adjoining the village hall — another place where you might park as an alternative to the pub. Having passed right-handed of the village hall, turn left between it and the school to follow a fenced footpath preceded by a vehicle barrier. This leads to a gravel farm road, which you cross to follow an unfenced path along an unploughed strip of grass across arable farmland: a commendable act and a striking example of a farmer who had put walkers first. The too seldom observed law (The Rights of Way Act 1990) requires that paths should be reinstated within 24 hours of ploughing, or within 14 days if it is the first disturbance for that crop. It is surely up to local authorities such as Hampshire County Council to take legal action and make an example of some of the more persistent offenders.

The field path ends at a stepped descent through a gap in a hedge to a narrow lane. Follow this right-handed, downhill to Dean, a remote and peaceful valley hamlet where weatherboarding, flint and thatch contribute their varied charms to a scene which time has altered very little. However

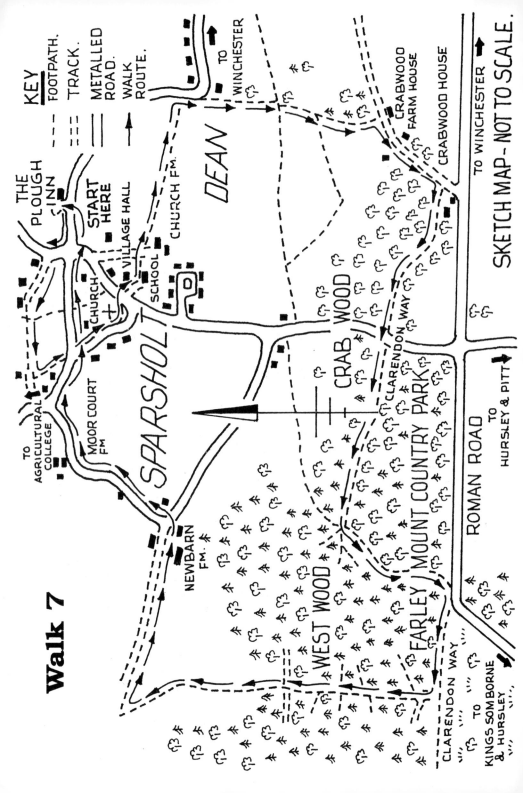

Walk 7

KEY
- – – – FOOTPATH.
- ▪ ▪ ▪ TRACK.
- ——— METALLED ROAD.
- ↑ WALK ROUTE.

THE PLOUGH INN

START HERE

VILLAGE HALL

CHURCH

SCHOOL

CHURCH FM.

MOOR COURT FM.

TO AGRICULTURAL COLLEGE

SPARSHOLT

DEAN

TO WINCHESTER

CRABWOOD FARM HOUSE

CRABWOOD HOUSE

TO WINCHESTER

CRAB WOOD

CLARENDON WAY

NEWBARN FM.

WEST WOOD

FARLEY MOUNT COUNTRY PARK

CLARENDON WAY

TO KINGS SOMBORNE & HURSLEY

ROMAN ROAD

TO HURSLEY & PITT

SKETCH MAP – NOT TO SCALE.

Unploughed strip left by farmer for the Sparsholt to Dean footpath

instead of straw-chewing, smock-clad peasants you are more likely to meet members of the green-welly brigade addressing each other, or possibly yourself, in cultured accents which owe very little to Hampshire dialect!

Where the metalled lane turns left at Dean, keep straight on to follow a footpath sensibly fenced from a muddy section of the adjacent bridleway. Hard going soon resumes, and path and bridleway unite to follow a common course uphill between bordering trees, a goodly number of which are the yews so much in evidence on the central Hampshire chalk, especially west of Winchester. At a staggered crossing of tree-hedged bridleways continue ahead, uphill, to where another bridleway turns right. Again, keep straight ahead, along the left-hand side of arable farmland. Undulating ground on all sides includes a steepish slope to your left on which an island of chalkland turf surrounds a central grove of yews and is surrounded in turn by ploughland — a thoroughly typical, pleasingly eyecatching assortment of downland scenery blending the products of man and nature.

Bushes briefly border your path, which descends a little before again climbing, with a woodland strip alongside it and a broad hillslope field to your right, rising to the eastern fringe of Crab Wood. At the top of the incline is Crabwood Farmhouse, near which you join and follow right-handed a metalled lane. Looking north from this, you can see Sparsholt church beyond intervening low ground, and Lainston House among trees fairly well to the right of it.

The hilltop lane leads you south-westward between pastureland and Crab Wood Nature Reserve, which lies to your right. Disregard paths turning right until you approach the end of Crab Wood, where you reach Farley Mount Country Park, as a sign alongside the road reminds you. Here you turn right to follow a timber-railed section of The Clarendon Way long distance walk, which links Winchester and Salisbury. This skirts some outbuildings and then a left-hand paddock before leading you through a corner of Crab Wood to reach the Hursley-Sparsholt road. Cross this to follow a continuation path which is also a bridleway and apt to be sticky, especially in winter. You will find stout footwear essential here, and a stick a very useful accessory.

Fencing to your left bounds a westerly section of Crab Wood largely set aside for walkers, with waymarked routes radiating from a car park and picnicking area adjoining the road which runs to the south of it. Oak and hazel predominate in what is preserved by Hampshire County Council, who now own it, as a tract of traditional woodland along with the characteristic flora and fauna of such habitat. Groves of larches and other conifers loom to your right as you head west, and the going becomes firmer as you approach a gateway at the boundary with the Forestry Commission's West Wood. On the near side of the gateway turn left to follow a firm path with deciduous Crab Wood to your left and West Wood's conifers beyond a fence to your right.

This brings you out on to a metalled section of the Roman road from Winchester to Old Sarum. Follow this right-handed to where the metalled road soon angles left, and from here continue straight ahead along the southern side of West Wood, with the open downland of Farley Mount Country Park rising to your left. Scattered birch, yew and other scrub patterns the otherwise spreading greensward which survives as an oasis of chalk downland as this used to be, thanks to its status as an open space for public recreation.

At the lowest point of the down turn right to pass a sign announcing your point of entry to West Wood. For a few yards you follow a gravel road, then where this turns left you follow a valley track ahead. Dense and sometimes dark conifer groves extend on either hand as you now head north to where a gateway precedes your emergence on to farmland. A widening tongue of

A delightful terrace of thatched cottages at Sparsholt

arable chalkland spreads beside the valley bridleway as you leave the woods behind you, presently angling slightly left towards a gateway through which you join an unmetalled road. I say 'unmetalled', but there are intermittent traces of long past efforts to macadamise at least some sections of it as this fence-bordered road leads you right-handed past some of the hedgeless land attached to Sparsholt College of Agriculture.

An uphill half-mile or more precedes farm buildings and redbrick dwellings around the point where the mainly unmetalled road reaches indisputable tarmac. At a fork here take the metalled road climbing left to return you to Sparsholt. Beyond Moor Court Farm a road from the agricultural college joins your own road from the left. Not many yards farther on you fork left to follow Home Lane. Flanked by a mixture of old thatched dwellings and modern 'executive homes', this ends at a four-way lane junction from which The Plough Inn appears just ahead, but from which you turn right to recover your transport if this was left in the village hall car park.

Meadows and Woods near Brambridge

WALK 8
At least **3 hours**
5 miles
Walk begins page 55

Background to the Walk

The prefix 'Bram' occurs in a number of placenames around the country and is said to refer to the presence of broom or brambles. We may therefore assume that Brambridge was a locality where broom (or brambles!) grew in some profusion near a bridge. Present day Brambridge consists of little more than a shop, The Dog and Crook pub, a cluster of neighbouring cottages and a few outlying dwellings. Chief among these latter is Brambridge House, now divided into flats, but once the home of Mrs. Fitzherbert, whom George IV secretly married.

Brambridge itself is now virtually part of Colden Common, which ceased to live up to its name when the common in question was enclosed in the 19th century. The amorphous residential area now so named has spread out in several directions, especially during the last few decades. Of greater note historically is nearby Bishopstoke, which dates from before the Norman Conquest. Recorded in Domesday as 'Stoches' and two centuries later as 'Stoke Episcopi', it means 'an outlying farmstead or hamlet belonging to the Bishop' —in this case, the Bishop of Winchester, one of the largest landholders in Hampshire. Stoke Park Wood remained ecclesiastical property until after World War II, when the Church Commissioners disposed of it by sale to the Forestry Commission. It is now very popular with recreational walkers, mainly from the immediate neighbourhood.

Maps
Landranger 1:50,000
Sheet 185
Pathfinder 1:25,000
Sheets SU 42/52 and
SU 41/51
Map Reference of
Start/Finish SU473217

How to get there
From Southampton follow A33 and M3 to the Eastleigh exit. From here follow A335 towards Eastleigh and then turn left at the first traffic lights to follow Woodside Avenue. Join and follow B3335 through Allbrook and Highbridge. After passing under the railway and crossing the Itchen, within half a mile turn right for Brambridge, where The Dog and Crook lies a few yards along on your right. A few yards farther on there is usually additional parking space in a service road on your right. There are

Walk 8

Distance : Allow 3 hours for this 5-mile walk.

From the pub follow the road past an adjacent weatherboarded barn and Brambridge Stores, then past a small terrace of brick cottages called The Crescent, directly beyond which you turn right to follow a fenced footpath. Within a few yards this path angles left and leads to a stile, which you cross to enter a paddock where horses graze. Follow the right-hand edge of this paddock to where the fence and hedge turn off at right-angles to your right and there continue ahead along a slightly raised grassy bank marking a former field boundary.

At the far left-hand corner of the paddock cross a stile to follow a path with a ditch to the left of it and a bushy area beyond. This brings you to another stile, beyond which your path, here well-defined, continues ahead with the ditch still to your left. You soon reach an unmetalled road leading to Lord's Wood, an area of scattered bungalows, sheds and caravans beginning immediately to your left. Cross a stile just ahead of you to follow a path which soon enters a riverside pasture; a bend of the Itchen lies to your right.

frequent trains and Solent Blue buses (service 48) between Southampton and Eastleigh, connecting with buses on Solent Blue service 44 between Stoke Common, Eastleigh and Winchester via Brambridge, Colden Common and Twyford.

Pub facilities
The Dog and Crook.
*Open all day on weekdays, this friendly village 'local' with a clientele from both near and far is a popular place of call for Itchen Valley walkers.
The Dog and Crook pub, like Topsy, has 'growed' with the passage of time from a small nucleus, thought to be at least 300 years old. It used to be owned by Isle of Wight brewers Mew Langton, who sold out to Strong and Co. of Romsey — taken over in their turn by Whitbread. Strong Country is one of three real ales on tap, the others being Flowers' Best and Whitbread's Traditional Draught Ale. A pub first and an eating house second, The Dog and Crook none the less offers a lunchtime menu*

ranging from brown bread sandwiches, jacket potatoes and ploughman's lunches to spaghetti bolognese, chilli, lasagne verdi, scampi, sausages, cheese burgers, home cooked gammon and egg and delicious steak and kidney pie. Food can be served in the evening by prior arrangement.

The clientele includes fishermen, riders and many other regulars from well outside the area. Its location near The Itchen Way attracts good numbers of walkers. The pub has been attractively modernised by making a single L-shaped bar area out of what used to be separate lounge and public bars. Pub-using walkers are welcome to use the pub car park, and children and dogs present no problem. Opening times are 1100-2300 on weekdays and the usual hours on Sundays. Lunchtime food may be ordered between 1200-1430.

Upon reaching the pasture, skirt around a wet patch before turning left to cross a stile and enter a wood of oaks and hazels.

A clearly defined path leads through this small wood and then out through a gap in a hedge where you join and follow right-ahead an unmade road serving bungaloid Lord's Wood. Ignore a straight road which soon turns right and keep straight on along a twisty hedged and fenced track. This becomes something between a narrow green lane and a path leading to a stile where you enter and cross a pasture in the direction indicated by a yellow waymarking arrow. A metal-barred stile precedes the Brambridge-Bishopstoke road, which you cross straight over. A stile with a step but no crossbars when I crossed it marks the start of a continuation path which follows the hedged leftward edge of a pasture to another stile.

Cross this and turn right, with the pasture hedgerow to your right. You then gradually veer away from the right-hand hedge to head for a stile clearly in view on the meadow's far side, in front of you. Having reached and crossed this, follow the leftward edge of the next pasture to a gate leading into a further pasture with a farmhouse in view just beyond it. Your footpath follows the left-hand edge of this pasture, turning left at first and then right with an expanse of woody and watery waste ground just over the fence to your left. Ignore a stile on your left preceding a path leading to the main road at Colden Common and carry on to a gate beyond which Leylands Farm and its outbuildings loom to your right.

Do not pass through this gate but turn right on its near side to continue along the left-hand side of the meadow, now heading south. This leads you downhill to a tree-fringed brook called Bow Lake, which does indeed broaden into a lake of sorts just to the left of where you cross it by a concrete bridge. The brook drains a much more substantial sheet of water, Fisher's Pond, an ancient fish

pond belonging to a mediaeval priestly college at Marwell Manor.

To cross the concrete bridge just mentioned I had to move aside part of a metal gate, stood on end against it to prevent livestock from straying from one side to the other. A yellow waymarking arrow here points your way uphill across the pasture south of the brook. Heading slightly right-handed of straight ahead, at the top of the incline you reach two stiles through a double fence. Do not cross these but turn left to follow the fence, soon reaching a stile alongside a metal gate at a narrow point between Upperbarn Copse, on your right, and Hill Copse, to your left. I sat on the stile to eat lunch while enjoying the northerly view across Bow Lake valley, where hedgerow trees hem pastures that spread towards the scattered dwellings of an area called Nob's Crook, beyond which woods march with the skyline.

After crossing this stile, follow the right-hand edge of successive paddocks, with Upperbarn Copse to your right. Two separate pairs of stiles flank plankless ditches which are not too deep to cross without undue effort and which I found to be almost dry. These are followed by two single stiles before you reach the far end of Upperbarn Copse, where you cross yet another stile alongside a gate on your right-hand side. The path beyond this passes a gateway into Woodland Trust-owned Upperbarn Copse and then becomes a fenced track along the left-hand edge of a field preceding a junction of tracks where you turn right to skirt another wood, Crowdhill Copse.

Here you have two alternatives. The first is to take a track that turns right through a swing-gate to follow a well-trodden course through the hardwoods and conifers of Crowdhill Copse. Like Upperbarn Copse, this was owned and replanted by the Forestry Commission before being purchased by the Woodland Trust for the public to enjoy. Keep to the main (and only) track until another track with a yellow waymarking arrow leads you right-

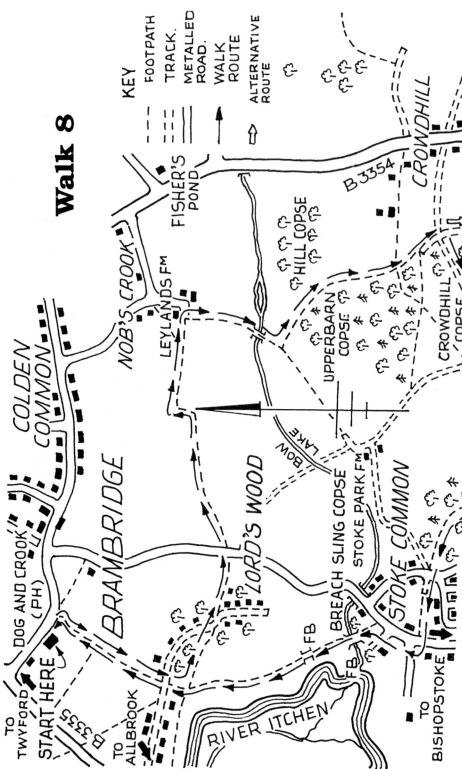

Walk 8

KEY

- – – – – FOOTPATH
- ·· ·· ·· TRACK.
- ——— METALLED ROAD.
- ↑ WALK ROUTE
- ⇨ ALTERNATIVE ROUTE

TO TWYFORD

DOG AND CROOK (PH)

START HERE

B 3335

TO ALLBROOK

COLDEN COMMON

NOB'S CROOK

FISHER'S POND

BRAMBRIDGE

LEYLANDS FM

HILL COPSE

B 3354

CROWDHILL

FAIR OAK

UPPERBARN COPSE

CROWDHILL COPSE

STOKE PARK W

LORD'S WOOD

BOW LAKE

BREACH SLING COPSE

STOKE PARK FM

STOKE COMMON

FB

FB

FB

RIVER ITCHEN

TO BISHOPSTOKE

SKETCH MAP – NOT TO SCALE

handed. In a dip you cross a stream by a plank bridge. Another plank, over a ditch, precedes a vehicle barrier beyond which you join and follow right-handed a bridleway between Stoke Park Wood and farmland which lies to your right.

The alternative route is not to enter Crowdhill Copse but to follow the track that leads past it to skirt the left-hand edge of another field. This brings you to the outskirts of Fair Oak, where you join a metalled road flanked by houses. Follow this road right-handed, soon reaching the eastern extremity of Stoke Park Wood, from which point a fenced bridleway leads you alongside the wood, with industrial land to your right. Open ground on that side precedes a crossing of tracks at the south-western end of Crowdhill Copse, which is now on your right once more. Carry straight on between Crowdhill Copse and Stoke Park Wood, across a gully where bridleway mud can be bypassed by climbing and following the right-hand bank of the track in question until firm going reasserts itself.

Where farmland appears on your right, the alternative sections of this walk reunite. Carry on along the fenced bridleway to where, at the first field's end, it turns right. From this point continue ahead along what now becomes just a footpath, with farmland still on your right-hand side and Stoke Park Wood on your left. This brings you to a vehicle barrier where your path enters Stoke Park Wood and climbs through a mixture of hardwoods and conifers to a track crossing where you turn right. Dark exotic firs, native oaks and lofty larches alternate along your way through this much walked wood on the outskirts of Bishopstoke, now a populous adjunct to Eastleigh and no longer the 'charming old village' noted by Moutray Read in 1908 when he wrote his book on Hampshire.

A green ride leads you through one of Stoke Park Wood's quieter corners to a stile, beyond which a well-defined path crosses a field towards the houses in view ahead. At the field's end cross a stile by a gate and join a track leading out on to Stoke Common Road, which you cross, facing half-right, and then follow unmetalled Jockey Lane. Continue from this along a footpath to join metalled Avington Close, leading to a T-junction with Dartington Road, which you follow left-handed to its own T-junction with the Bishopstoke-Brambridge road.

Follow the latter right-handed past a telephone kiosk and two lodge cottages on your left. Where the metalled path on your left ends, turn left through a vehicle barrier to leave the road and follow a path between a left-hand shrubbery and some paddocks on your right. Where the paddocks end your path briefly angles right before making a stepped descent through a steepish part of a wood called Breach Sling Copse. Where the gradient slackens the footpath seems to divide. If you keep right-handed it resumes a stepped descent through birches and hollies to cross a brook by a concrete bridge.

A well-defined meadow path now leads you north to a plank bridge over a brook in the midst of pastures flanking the east bank of the Itchen, which comes into view from time to time. Keep straight on to pass through a gap beside the remnants of an old metal stile into a second pasture, then through another gap into a third pasture. At the far end of this the path divides. Follow the one that bears right-handed of a house in grounds surrounded by a board fence. This leads to a stile which you will recognise having crossed on the outward journey. Cross it again and the unmade road to Lord's Wood that lies just beyond it to follow a streamside path to a stile, then beside the same stream (more of a ditch) to another stile. This precedes the horse paddock you first encountered and which you now recross to reach the stile on its far side. Beyond this the fenced final few yards of your path lead to Brambridge, where you started. The Dog and Crook is just round the corner!

Waterside Ways and Field Paths near Shawford

Background to the Walk

First recorded as 'Scaldeforda' in 1208, Shawford means simply 'shallow ford'. Today it consists of little besides a pub, a couple of shops, a railway station and a few scattered private dwellings including Shawford House, a beautiful stone building dating from 1685 surrounded by timbered parkland bracketed by arms of the Itchen.

Shawford and Twyford lie on opposite sides of the river, with Twyford's Church of St. Mary forming a prominent landmark across the watermeadows. Twyford church was rebuilt in 1876-7 but the font and round pillars and capitals of the nave arcades are retained from its predecessor. Twelve so-called Druid stones were found under the original Norman tower. Local tradition links these with Twyford's first Christian church having possibly been built on the site of a Druidical temple. Details of village history displayed inside the church include mention of there having been six mills and pasturage for 15 swine, the whole worth £15 a year, at the time of Domesday. Twyford Manor was then part of the Bishop of Winchester's demesne. In 1551 Edward VI took the manor into his own hands prior to giving it to Sir Henry Seymour of Marwell, his uncle. A leading family for several centuries were the Mildmays, Sir Henry Mildmay having been a great favourite of Charles I. There is still a Mildmay House, close to the church on the route of this walk.

Maps
Landranger 1:50,000 Sheet 185
Pathfinder 1:25,000 Sheet SU 42/52
Map Reference of Start/Finish SU473250

How to get there
From Southampton follow A33 and M3 north to Compton interchange, then follow the signposted route to Shawford, which doubles round under the motorway to reach your destination by way of B3386. A side road between the railway bridge and The Bridge Hotel gives access to the pub's car park and also has space alongside it for parking. Shawford station is served hourly by stopping trains between Southampton and Winchester.

Pub facilities
The Bridge Hotel
thrives on quality home cooking which brings customers from London as well as Southampton. Food is served between 1200-1400 and 1900-2130 seven days a week. Pub hours are 1100-1430 and 1800-2300 on weekdays, except in summer, when the pub remains open all day. Sunday opening hours are as usual. A large selection of draught beers and lagers complements a choice of three real ales. There are weekly barbecues in summer, and children's play areas indoors and out make this a popular family pub. Dogs only admitted to the garden in summer. Walkers using the pub may use the car park.
The Captain Barnard
at Otterbourne is a roomy, ultra-modern hostelry with a name derived from local history. Captain Barnard was a soldier in Cromwell's army when the Civil War raged in Hampshire. His pub serves food seven days a week between 1200-2200, the pub itself being open all day, with the

Otterbourne is a name devoid of any shred of mystery except the present whereabouts of the otters which once hunted eels along the said bourne. My only glimpse of a wild otter was on the Itchen, way back in the '50s, but you would be very lucky today to spot one of these lithe and lovely animals in any part of Hampshire.

The village of Otterbourne is strung out along a road first built by the Romans to link Winchester (Venta Belgarum) with Southampton or, rather, Clausentum (over the river at Bitterne). Lands here were given by King Edgar in the 10th century to the Bishops of Winchester. Until Otterbourne's Church of St. Matthew was rebuilt by Keble in a more central village location in 1837-9, parishioners walked to a 13th century place of worship quite close to the Itchen, east of the village. Most of this was demolished when the new church took its place, though the chancel still stood until long afterwards. The site of the church is still delineated but no other trace remains, the graveyard being preserved as a nature reserve and a place of sanctity by Otterbourne Conservation Group.

At two separate stages of this walk you will follow the one-time towpath of the Itchen Navigation. This was a canalised stretch of the River Itchen which once carried barge traffic between Southampton and Winchester. Conveyance of goods by this route involved transhipment at Woodmill, where the freshwater river joins the tidal estuary, and the negotiation of locks separating different levels of the artificial waterway, remnants of which are still in place. The barges, of course, were horse-drawn, and the haul upstream to the terminal point, below Wharf Hill at Winchester, was a time-consuming process which survived less than 30 years after the coming of the railway to Southampton in 1839-40.

usual hours on Sunday except for restaurant customers, who may order drinks with their meal at any time. The emphasis here is on value for money. Flowers' Original and Strong Country real ales are always on tap as well as a good selection of wines. Walkers who wish to start here instead of at Shawford and who first check with the management may leave their cars in the pub car park.

Walk 9

Distance: Allow up to 3 hours for this walk of about 5 miles.

From The Bridge Hotel at Shawford head east to cross the old Itchen Navigation as you follow the footway bordering B3386. Walled and timbered parkland conceals Shawford House on your right as you make your way towards a right-hand bend of the road where you turn left by a footpath sign to follow a concreted field-edge path. This soon angles right as a well-defined earth path to cross a river valley pasture. The stubby spire of Twyford church probes up from trees beyond the meadows as you now head for a concrete footbridge which takes you over a shallow side channel of the Itchen.

After crossing this bear right along the edge of the pasture beyond to reach and cross a bridge over the River Itchen proper. A path-cum-track leads on ahead from here to where Twyford church lies to your right. I found the church open and went in to have a look at those Norman arcades which were embodied in the present place of worship when rebuilt in Victorian times. Of special antiquity and fame is the churchyard yew, reputedly 1,000 years old and possibly the oldest clipped yew in any English churchyard.

Leaving the church, pass three-storeyed Mildmay House on your right as you head north to follow narrow Church Lane. Delightful Itchen Valley views precede the walled grounds of Twyford Lodge on your left as you follow one of the most charming village backwaters of Twyford, set well

Weir by the old mill at Shawford

apart from the traffic bustle of the main thoroughfare, B3335. This you reach at Church Lane's northern end where you immediately turn left to follow a hedged, unmetalled lane down to a bridge over an old mill-race. No doubt a predecessor of the disused mill which lies to your left here was one of the half-dozen Twyford boasted at the time of the Domesday Survey.

Cross a stile to follow the fenced left edge of an Itchen Valley pasture where tall trees, some of them ivy-clustered, dot the level riverine landscape. After crossing a cattle bridge over a side stream your path is kept above normal flood-water level by old railway sleepers as it leads you across a wet stretch of the pasture immediately following. Beyond a second cattle bridge turn sharp right to cross a stile by Compton Lock, one of the points along the course of the old Itchen Navigation where horse-drawn barges had to wait while the water level was adjusted.

You now turn left to follow the towpath, with the waterway to your right and a screening fringe of trees to your left. A concreted bridge over an old mill-race precedes your point of re-emergence on to the Twyford-Shawford road, B3386, which you follow right-handed back past The Bridge Hotel, where you started, and under the railway arch beyond. You then immediately turn left to follow a path from which another soon leads you right-handed, stepped in places as it climbs Shawford Down, a county-owned open space. At a high point on this is a stone memorial to the dead of two world wars. From there you can look back across the broad vale of the Itchen towards the gentle folds of the downlands east of Twyford, while at the foot of the slope Shawford's red brick peeps out between trees which flank the railway.

Carry on south-westward over Shawford Down, where your path joins another to emerge through trees on to the stub-end of a cul-de-sac. This leads within yards to a metalled estate road which you follow left-ahead

Compton Lock, near Shawford

between the luxury homes of South Down, many of which enjoy prime positions overlooking the Itchen Valley. The first right-turning road, Cross Way, ends at a T-junction with Fairfield Road, which you follow left to Grove Road. Follow the latter right-handed to join Winchester Road at the southern end of Compton, opposite The Captain Barnard pub and restaurant. Follow what started as a Roman road south, downhill, past where the A31 turns right and on, ahead, over the Otter Bourne, one of the Itchen's lesser tributaries. How many years ago was it, I wonder, when an otter last ventured this way?

Continue into Otterbourne village for only a few yards more before turning left through the forecourt and car park of The Old Forge Restaurant, directly beyond the building itself. At the far end of the car park cross a stile on your right and climb the meadow beyond, heading diagonally away from the right-hand edge of it. Beyond a swing-gate at the top of a slight incline you enter a second meadow where your path angles slightly left and descends to a stile and so out on to metalled Kiln Lane, which leads from Otterbourne to Brambridge.

Follow this leftward round a couple of bends to a footpath sign on your left, preceding a stile and a path through the graveyard of Otterbourne old church. Lichened tombstones reveal burials dating back to at least the early 18th century, while the site of the church itself is marked out by stones to the left of the path. The graveyard, as already mentioned, nowadays serves as a nature sanctuary and is maintained as such by village conservationists from Otterbourne. At the far end of it cross a stile to follow a clearly-defined path along the right-hand edge of a meadow, on a converging course with the railway on its tree-clad embankment to your right.

The rattle and rush of electric trains and the throb of their diesel-hauled counterparts punctuates the rural peace of the latter stages of this walk. Somehow, though, one minds these sounds less than the traffic noises to

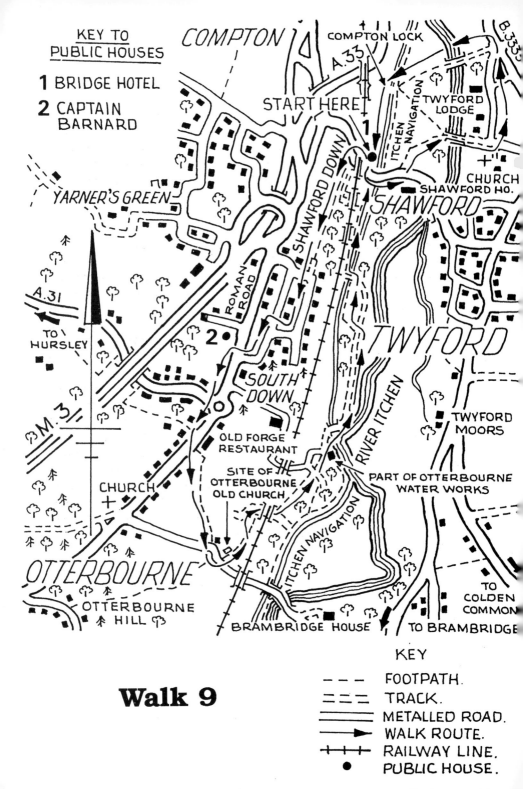

KEY TO
PUBLIC HOUSES

1 BRIDGE HOTEL
2 CAPTAIN
BARNARD

COMPTON

COMPTON LOCK

B.3335

A.33

START HERE

ITCHEN NAVIGATION

TWYFORD
LODGE

YARNER'S GREEN

SHAWFORD DOWN

CHURCH
SHAWFORD HO.

SHAWFORD

A.31

TO
HURSLEY

ROMAN ROAD

TWYFORD

M.3

2

SOUTH
DOWN

RIVER ITCHEN

TWYFORD
MOORS

CHURCH

OLD FORGE
RESTAURANT

SITE OF
OTTERBOURNE
OLD CHURCH

PART OF OTTERBOURNE
WATER WORKS

ITCHEN NAVIGATION

OTTERBOURNE

OTTERBOURNE
HILL

BRAMBRIDGE HOUSE

TO BRAMBRIDGE

TO
COLDEN
COMMON

Walk 9

KEY

– – – FOOTPATH.
≡≡≡ TRACK.
═══ METALLED ROAD.
———► WALK ROUTE.
+++ RAILWAY LINE.
• PUBLIC HOUSE.

be endured wherever a country walk impinges upon almost any metalled road.

Two further stiles precede a brick arch via which the farm road you briefly join here takes you underneath the railway. Directly beyond this you cross a stile on your left to follow a well-defined, raised grass path to another stile which you cross near the far right-hand corner of the next meadow. A fenced path leads to a cinder track, beyond which you cross another stile, then a paddock, followed by a further stile. This precedes a macadamised driveway approach to one of the Otterbourne Waterworks buildings, which you cross to follow a gravel track.

Within yards this joins the Itchen Navigation towpath, the original route of which is briefly left by The Itchen Way public footpath which nowadays makes use of it. After bridging the Navigation and passing a tree in a right-hand meadow on which a sign mysteriously warns walkers to 'beware of the asps' — a slightly less confrontational way of saying 'keep out'? — you follow a fenced grass-and-gravel track with fields on both sides of it. A stile precedes more of the same as far as a gate, on the near side of which you cross a stile on your left, beyond which a fenced path leads to the Navigation's east bank, which you now follow north.

After crossing a stile and a bridge over the Navigation by farm buildings, you cross another stile, on your right, to continue north with the canalised waterway now on your right. Where your path soon joins a macadamised lane, follow this straight on to where a small terrace of cottages comes into view ahead. At this point bear right to resume a grass path. This joins a tarmac path serving the cottages, which you follow right-ahead, with frequent small bridges spanning a water channel which separates the path from cottage gardens on your left, while the Navigation winds to your right. This brings you out on to B3386, which you follow left-handed for a few yards back to where you started at Shawford.

Over the Downs near Twyford

WALK 10

Allow **3 hours**

6 miles

Walk begins page 69

Background to the Walk

Twyford, meaning 'two fords', has been called a gem among Hampshire villages. If a narrow main street with much traffic lessens its gemlike appeal to some, efforts to re-route heavy goods vehicles via the M3 \ M27 have helped to preserve the old world charm of a valley settlement whose story began more than a thousand years ago.

At the time of Domesday there were six mills on the Itchen, west of the village, from which the view today across watermeadows towards the church demands a Constable to paint it. However, the Church of St. Mary as we see it today is not ancient, having been rebuilt in 1876-7 whilst retaining almost nothing of its mediaeval predecessor except the font and arcades to the nave. The churchyard yew was mentioned in Domesday and its appearance matches its age. Until expelled for writing satirical verse about his teachers, the poet Alexander Pope had a brief spell of schooling at Seagar's Buildings, near the present-day Seagar's Farm. A happier claim to educational fame attaches to Twyford School, founded in the early 19th century and thought to be the oldest preparatory school in England.

Owslebury's Church of St. Andrew dates from the 13th century when it was in the care of priests from a monastic establishment at Marwell. The Early English building underwent alterations during the reign of Charles II, as we are reminded by a stone bearing the date 1675 on the west side

Maps
Landranger 1:50,000
Sheet 185
Pathfinder 1:25,000
Sheet SU 42/52
Map Reference of
Start/Finish SU481243

How to get there
From Southampton follow A33 and M3 to Chandler's Ford interchange. Follow A335 towards Eastleigh and turn left at the first traffic lights to follow Woodside Avenue north, continuing along B3335 from Allbrook and past Brambridge into Twyford, where Park Lane is the first turning right, by The Bugle Inn. The Phoenix Inn is a few yards farther along the main road, on your left, while The Dolphin is on your right as you turn right into Hazeley Road at the village centre traffic lights. Buses on Solent Blue Line service 48 from Southampton connect

at Eastleigh with those on service 44 between Stoke Common and Winchester via Twyford, and Hampshire Bus service 69 between Southsea and Winchester via Fareham and Bishop's Waltham passes through Twyford. There are also frequent trains between Southampton and Eastleigh.

Pub facilities
The Bugle Inn.
Recently extensively refurbished, this Eldridge Pope house specialises in good food covering the whole range from light snacks and home-made pies to T-bone steaks, prepared in an ultra-modern kitchen. The large bar has some 25 tables and serves a good range of real ales and draught lagers. Walkers who ask first may use the pub car park.
The Phoenix Inn.
A 17th century inn, this Marston house has ship's timbers and an inglenook fireplace as part of its structure. A skittle alley, beer garden and large car park are other features, as are traditional ales and good pub grub including vegetarian

of the tower. It was restored in 1890, very largely on the initiative of the then Earl of Northesk, who lived at nearby Longwood House, a mansion now demolished. I found the church locked but a notice indicated where the key could be borrowed.

The county's last working windmill remained in use at Owslebury until the late 19th century. There was also a windpump to draw water from a well deep in the chalk to supply the needs of those who lived in this second highest Hampshire village, whose name is probably more often mispronounced than any other. Call it 'Usselbury' and nobody will have cause to contradict you. According to placename pundits it means the stronghold of someone called Osla, or perhaps a haunt of the ousel, a near relative of the blackbird.

Walk 10

Distance: Allow 3 hours for this walk of not quite 6 miles.

With a flint wall at first to your right, and redbrick cottages to your left after leaving The Bugle Inn behind you, follow Park Lane gently uphill, heading in an easterly direction. After passing close to where a Roman villa site was discovered in 1891, the lane sloughs off surrounding dwellings to give right-hand views towards downy hill-slope pastures to the south. Where the metalled lane soon bears right, fork left to follow a hedge-bordered gravelly road. With an ivied bank topped by trees to your right and valley views towards Twyford's church and more rising ground to your left, this leads to another metalled lane, beyond which you cross a stile straight ahead and an arable field beyond.

Valley views to your left continue as you follow a fairly well-defined public footpath to a gap in a wire fence ahead, with a stile to the left of it. You now cross a dip and then rise to a further stile, specials. Walkers may use the pub car park subject to checking that space is available.

The Dolphin.
Another Marston house, this is more of a village 'local', with a car park at the rear which walkers may use, but please ask first. There is a beer garden and facilities for pub games such as darts and pool. Traditional beers go with quality pub food at reasonable prices.

The Ship Inn (Pictured top right)
This friendly Owslebury hostelry has a reputation for good food and choice ales. Children are welcome and a play area is provided. Walkers starting here may use the pub car park if using the pub.

beyond which you join and follow right-handed a gently rising, fenced green lane. Alongside the fence are hedgerow remnants which presently merge to become continuous hedges flanking your unmetalled byway, which curves steadily left-handed while a grassy ridge looms to your right with a line of trees along its crest.

Ivied trees to your right precede a padlocked metal gate around which you can walk to join and follow right-handed a narrow, metalled lane. Yews and beeches shade your descent to Hazelwood Farm, just after passing which you cross Hensting Lane and then almost immediately turn left where a footpath sign points your way through a gap in the hedge. You now head diagonally away from the right-hand hedgerow as you cross an arable field where I found the path not to have been reinstated. Pass through a gap in the hedgerow ahead to cross another arable field towards the bottom end of a line of trees and scrub, which latter flanks your path on your right as you continue ahead, uphill. Your path bends left for a few yards before climbing a bank to a double stile without steps, after crossing which you follow the right-hand edge of a fenced paddock to another stepless stile preceding a fenced final few yards to where your footpath joins the road in Owslebury village.

Turn right here and cross the road, passing the old flint-walled village schoolhouse as you approach St. Andrew's Church. The 'prohibitively high cost of insuring unlocked churches' is stated as the reason for your having to ask for a key at a house called The Granary if you want to look inside.

Owslebury church

Ancient graffiti in the stonework at the main entrance suggest that vandalism was rampant long before spray-paint cans were invented.

Returning to the main village road, follow it left-handed past cottages of flint, thatch and beams to where The Ship Inn lies to your right by the bus turn-round point from which the road turns left for Marwell. Beyond the pub, carry on past where a lane called White Hill turns right and then fork left by a sign for a house called Longfields to follow a bridleway. Not many yards along the latter fork right where a sign indicates a tree-bordered track as a public footpath.

Preceded by a rusty metal gate, this leads to a second gate and then on through to a third flanked by a stile, which you cross to enter a downland hill-slope pasture. As you follow the left-hand edge of this you can look to your right across the tree-hedged Hensting Valley to downlands beyond: one of several notable chalk country panoramas on this walk. Cross or walk around the next stile, which I found to be broken, and carry on along the fenced upper edge of the downland pasture beyond it. After crossing the next stile — with or without the broken step I encountered — head diagonally right-handed from the left-hand fence beyond, on a converging course with a tree hedge, towards a gap through which you pass by another broken stile.

Follow the tree-hedged upper edge of the pasture beyond, still heading south-westward. Beyond the next stile head diagonally right across another pasture, on the far side of which, with farm buildings in view below you to your right, you cross yet another stile. Continue ahead across the arable field that now confronts you, where I found the path had not been reinstated after ploughing. With luck other walkers will have trodden out the route of it, which ends at another stile with a stepped descent into a hollow, hedged 'green' lane. Turn right here to join the Fisher's Pond-Owslebury road, which you follow right-ahead for a few yards before crossing a stile on your left.

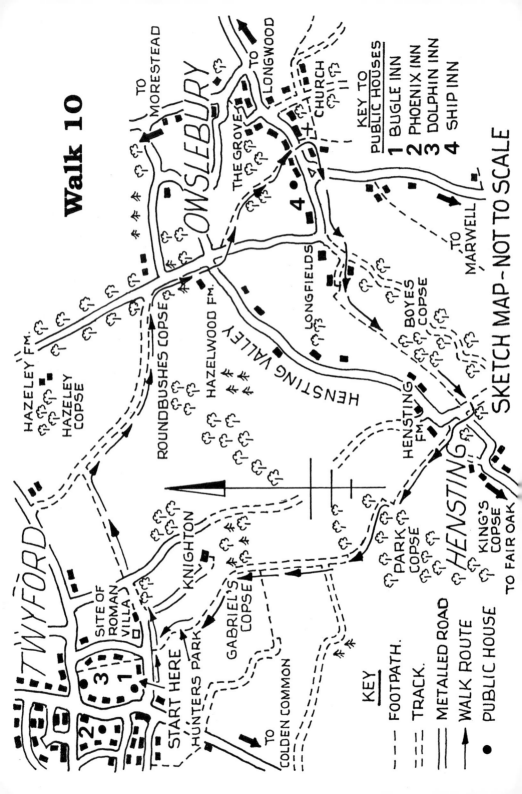

Walk 1O

TWYFORD

OWSLEBURY

HENSTING

SKETCH MAP ~ NOT TO SCALE

TO MORESTEAD

TO LONGWOOD

CHURCH

KEY TO
PUBLIC HOUSES
1 BUGLE INN
2 PHOENIX INN
3 DOLPHIN INN
4 SHIP INN

THE GROVE

HAZELEY FM.

HAZELEY COPSE

ROUNDBUSHES COPSE

HAZELWOOD FM.

HENSTING VALLEY

LONGFIELDS

HENSTING FM.

BOYES COPSE

TO MARWELL

SITE OF ROMAN VILLA

KNIGHTON

HUNTERS PARK

START HERE

GABRIEL'S COPSE

PARK COPSE

KING'S COPSE

TO FAIR OAK

TO COLDEN COMMON

KEY
--- FOOTPATH.
=== TRACK.
━━ METALLED ROAD
→ WALK ROUTE
● PUBLIC HOUSE

Green lane between Twyford and Owslebury

You now follow a footpath along the right-hand edge of three paddocks, with Hensting Farm's buildings, including an old tithe barn, directly to your right. Beyond a fourth stile — counting the one where you left the road — you follow the left-hand edge of some arable ground, with a line of trees and a derelict chalk pit to your left. A few yards beyond the point where the field edge bends right, a stepless stile on your left precedes a footpath, hedged at first and then fenced on the left, with an arable field separating it from woodland to your left. This leads you to an old stile flanked by a gate, beyond which your path coincides with a farm track.

Beyond a crossing of tracks a field's length ahead you skirt left-handed of a medium-sized wood called Gabriel's Copse, with arable farmland to your left. At the far end of the copse the farm track you have been following up to this point dips right-handed but your footpath bears slightly left. Trees clothe a bank to your left as the path diagonally descends, with a dry chalk valley on your right. This brings you to Twyford's sports field, Hunters Park, across which you head diagonally right-handed towards its exit and so out into Park Lane, which you follow left-handed back to your starting point.

Itchen Valley Footpaths around Easton

WALK 11
Allow **2 hours**
4 miles
Walk begins page 76

Background to the Walk

Easton is one of those mellow villages that time has largely passed by. Almost a mile from the nearest main road, its lanes carry little wheeled traffic to disturb the peace of a community largely housed in old world cottages of outstanding picturesqueness. Cultivated chalkland undulates gently to the south, its smooth contours complementing the level, willow-patterned pastures of the upper Itchen Valley, alongside which the village slumbers.

The placename 'Easton' dates from Saxon times and means simply, 'the eastern village' and refers to its geographical relationship to Winchester. Domesday tells us that the manor was held by the Bishop. The prior and monks of St. Swithun's of the same city were principal tenants of land at Easton for several centuries before Henry VIII's Dissolution. Perhaps the most famous lord of the manor was soldier-poet Sir Philip Sidney, who died heroically in battle in the Low Countries during the reign of Elizabeth I. Precisely where the old manor house was is uncertain, but following its demolition 200 years ago some materials were re-used in the reconstruction of Dymoke House, on the route of this walk.

Approached by way of a lych gate commemorating those who died in the First World War, Easton's Church of St. Mary was built between 1120 and 1170. Its flint walls and the magnificent Norman arch surmounting its south doorway combine to

Maps
Landranger 1:50,000
Sheet 185
Pathfinder 1:25,000
Sheet SU 43/53
Map Reference of
Start/Finish SU513321

How to get there
From Southampton head north along the A33 and M3 to Winchester bypass. At next interchange beyond Hockley traffic lights filter left to join Alton-bound A31, from which you take the lane leading north at the roundabout where A31 is joined from the left by the B3404 (Alresford Road) from Winchester. The Percy Hobbs pub lies to your right as you join the lane, which you follow for 2 miles to reach Easton. Solent Bus service 47 from Southampton connects at Winchester on weekdays with Alder Valley Bus service 214

exemplify the building's great age as you view it from the road, although its apsidal eastern end may be older still. The distinctive steeple was remodelled in its present form during restoration in the 1860s. Early Norman lancet windows along the north wall of the nave admit limited light, with the result that the church has a rather dark interior.

Easternmost of four placenames suffixed 'Worthy', from a Saxon word meaning 'place' or 'hamlet', nearby Martyr Worthy clusters around a cul-de-sac running south from the King's Worthy-Alresford road to the Itchen. How the prefix 'Martyr' came to be chosen seems uncertain, though records tell of a John la Martre having links with this place in the 13th century. From then until the Dissolution the manor was held by St. Swithun's of Winchester, a link recalled by the dedication of the church at Martyr Worthy, built around 1150 on the site of a possible Saxon predecessor which may have been an uncertainly located second church mentioned in Domesday as having belonged to Easton. Like its counterpart at Easton, Martyr Worthy church has an eyecatching Norman south doorway and another on its north side with particularly striking decoration. Inside, by command of Elizabeth I, an edict confirmed later by Charles II, the Ten Commandments are spelt out for all to see on the side of the chancel arch facing the nave.

Chilland lies on its own quiet cul-de-sac and lacks a church. Its name is aid to be a corruption of Ceoliglond, meaning 'Ship Island', which might refer to a long lost port of call for craft plying the Itchen when the river, according to some, was navigable as far upstream as Alresford for a time in the Middle Ages. Another school of thought maintains that this was never possible. Chilland Mill survived until the turn of the century and was used for milling cattle fodder for local farmers.

between Winchester and Old Alresford, which passes within a mile of Easton at the first right-hand turning after crossing the M3 east of Abbots Worthy. Alder Valley buses are replaced on Sundays by Oakley Coaches service 453 between Winchester and Aldershot. On Thursdays only, Gemini Travel operate a limited service (number 94) between Winchester Broadway and Easton.

Pub facilities
The Cricketers Inn.
A free house with facilities for children. Good choice of real ales on offer. Food is served seven days a week, lunchtimes and evenings and includes a Sunday roast, served between 1200 and 1400. Dogs on leads are admitted and walkers using pub may use the car park.
The Chestnut Horse.
An ancient farmhouse, with a history dating back to c.1520 and long-established as a pub. A free house with a good range of brews, facilities for children and a good restaurant, food being served seven days a week,

lunch and evenings.
Walkers using pub
may use the car park.

Walk 11

Distance: Allow 2 hours for this 4-mile walk, plus an extra hour for leisurely river-watching and visiting churches.

We parked alongside the road that turns right when you reach Easton village centre, a little way short of a leftward bend preceding The Chestnut Horse. From here walk back to the crossroads by The Cricketers Inn where you turn right. Then, after a few yards, turn left to follow a 'no through road'. To the left of this is Dymoke House.

Opposite is Easton churchyard, with the 12th century Church of St. Mary framed by greenery as you look north across a typical cross-section of the upper Itchen Valley. Churchyard yews are accompanied by a fine specimen of a locust tree, a native to North America which farmer-author William Cobbett recommended (unsuccessfully) to British foresters as a profitable investment.

Just beyond the churchyard turn right, then immediately left through an iron swing-gate into a north-sloping meadow with a public seat alongside it. Head diagonally right-handed towards the north-west end of this meadow, where you cross a stile and continue ahead in a direct line across another field to a further stile. Beyond this your path soon becomes hedged on both sides as it heads west towards the M3 motorway, which you pass under by a pedestrian tunnel parallel with one of the arms of the Itchen.

Your well-used path emerges from bordering trees into the terminal end of a lane separated by a gate from the grounds of a riverside house on your right. A prominent notice here warns walkers of legal provisions laid down for the guidance of those who use public footpaths through private property.

Having pondered these points, cross the lane as if intending to follow the footpath that leads on beyond it in a south-westerly direction. Hardly will you have stepped on to this path than you turn right to follow another path which bypasses the gate last mentioned and continues through the private grounds of a house which was once a fulling mill. Such mills operated a water-powered means of processing cloth by saturating it in soap and water, then twisting, rolling and shrinking it to produce a felt-like material.

Having resisted temptation to linger, cross the Itchen by footbridges to follow a path that heads north-east through luxuriant river valley vegetation before bridging another arm of the Itchen and emerging into a cul-de-sac at the lower end of Abbots Worthy. Pass through a kissing-gate on your

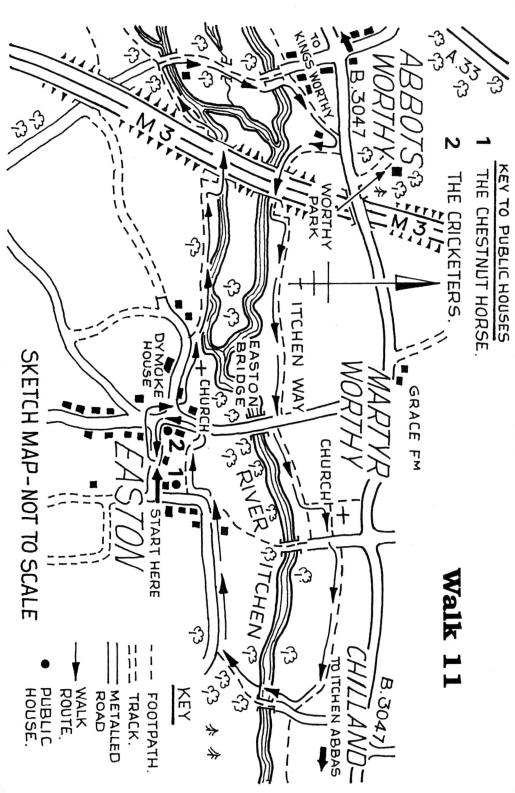

Walk 11

KEY TO PUBLIC HOUSES

1 THE CHESTNUT HORSE.

2 THE CRICKETERS.

SKETCH MAP—NOT TO SCALE

KEY

- - - - FOOTPATH.
═ ═ ═ TRACK.
════ METALLED ROAD.
↓ WALK ROUTE.
● PUBLIC HOUSE.

A.33

M 3

ABBOTS WORTHY

B.3047

TO KINGS WORTHY

WORTHY PARK

MARTYR WORTHY

GRACE FM

ITCHEN WAY

EASTON BRIDGE

CHURCH

DYMOKE HOUSE

EASTON

START HERE

RIVER ITCHEN

CHURCH

CHILLAND

B.3047

TO ITCHEN ABBAS

right here to follow a path that then heads diagonally left, steering what we found to be a well-defined course through lush summer herbage and bearing slightly away from the river with its bordering trees. After skirting a building, your path enters a field which it crosses, diagonally left, in line with the route of it up to this point, to reach the King's Worthy-Alresford road, B3047, over a stile.

Follow the road right-handed for a few yards past the grounds of a private dwelling, then cross a stile to enter the next field on your right. The right-hand verge of this is followed by a path waymarked here, and elsewhere, as The Itchen Way, a route mapped out by Richard Kenchington, Eastleigh Group chairman of the Ramblers' Association, and leading all the way between the Itchen's headwaters and its outflow.

Fenced on the right and then on the left, with Worthy Park mansion in view on higher ground to the left and then behind you, your footpath burrows back under the M3 motorway to follow field margins in an easterly direction, with the Itchen Valley to your right. Easton church looms beyond the river's several arms as you approach a lane which you follow briefly right-handed and then cross, with Martyr Worthy's Church of St. Swithun showing its steeple above treetops left-ahead.

After following the right-hand edge of the second field beyond the lane, when you reach this field's far end turn left to follow another field-edge path from which a fenced path soon turns right. This joins a driveway which you follow ahead into a road along which you turn left, with Martyr Worthy church to your left.

Opposite the church follow a driveway with a half-hidden public footpath sign on your right at the start of it and thatched cottages lying back behind gardens on the same side. Where the drive soon bends right a field-edge footpath leads straight on, giving good views across the Itchen Valley towards rising farmland and the billowing treetops of a fairly substantial wood away on the south side of the river. Your path presently bends right to follow a fenced and tree-lined course to Chilland, another sequestered Itchenside hamlet served by a quiet cul-de-sac.

Follow the latter right-handed past what used to be Chilland Mill, beyond which a well-used, tree-fringed path leads you south-west after bridging the river. This brings you out on to the Avington-Easton lane, a byway little used by motor traffic which you follow right-handed for half a mile back into Easton. A right-turning footpath along the east side of The Chestnut Horse leads to another road, which you follow, left-handed back into the village to where you started. The Cricketers Inn is just ahead here, at the crossroads.

Two Walks from the Bush Inn, Ovington

WALK 12
1 or **2/3 hours**
1·5 or **4 miles**
Walk begins page 81

Background to the Walks

Avington, Yavington, Lovington and Ovington are all found along a three-mile stretch of the upper Itchen Valley. This is a part of Hampshire which preserves the peace and charm of bygone times to an extent which may be measured by reading the writings of those who knew it when motor cars and mechanised agriculture had cast no blemish upon the fair face of the south country. One such author was D. H. Moutray Read, whose *Highways and Byways in Hampshire* hit the bookstalls in 1908. His enthusiastic evocation of this ageless riverine world, with its crystalline, many-channelled waters meandering through summer pastures where cattle graze belly-deep in the herbage, conjures up a scene just as I enjoyed it when I sampled these two walks.

As for those intriguing placenames, only two of them identify present day villages. As centres of population, Yavington and Lovington have shrunk over the centuries to the point where the Ordnance Survey map disregards them both. Avington and Ovington still merit village status, but whereas both lack shops and the former has not even a pub, Ovington is less seriously disadvantaged.

Ovington's few cottages once housed the local farming community but are now largely the homes of those whose workaday world is elsewhere. Its little Church of St. Peter was rebuilt in its present form in the 1860s, at a time when church restoration was rampant in neighbouring parishes and

Maps
Landranger 1:50,000
Sheet 185
Pathfinder 1:25,000
Sheet SU 43/53
Map Reference of
Start/Finish SU561318

How to get there
From Southampton follow A33 and M3 to Winchester bypass. Not far beyond Hockley traffic lights filter left to join A31, follow this towards Alresford. About 5 miles along A31 turn left at a crossroads to follow a downhill lane to Ovington, at the lower end of which turn left to The Bush Inn. There are overflow parking facilities along the adjacent road. Solent Blue Bus service 47 from Southampton connects at Winchester with Alder Valley Bus service 214 between Winchester and Old Alresford, which passes within a mile of Ovington along the

King's Worthy-Alresford road, B3047. On Sundays this service is replaced by Oakley Coaches service 253 between Winchester and Aldershot. Alight by the village green at Itchen Stoke to start and end the two Walks here instead of at Ovington.

Pub facilities
The Bush Inn.

Far from being a mere village pub, The Bush Inn draws its clientele from all over the county. Indeed, people come here from the far corners of the world. One recent visitor from across the Atlantic turned out to be a personal friend of President Bush, who afterwards wrote a treasured letter of acknowledgment to the owners of his name-sake free house in the heart of Hampshire. Dating from the 17th century, the tucked-away riverside hostelry relies on much more than its idyllic rural setting to keep the customers flocking in. As well as a choice of selected real ales, there is an extensive wine list combining quality with value. The

indeed throughout much of the country. The wheel at Ovington Mill still whirred to help bring music to the ear of Moutray Read in Edwardian times, but has long fallen silent, while the mill house, with its brick walls and leadlight windows looking as spick and span as ever, survives as a private residence.

Itchen Stoke, just across the river, derives part of its name from its having been a secondary settlement to nearby Itchen Abbas. Itchen Stoke clusters around a village green overlooked from just across Water Lane, to the east, by a cottage built from exceptionally large flints, once the village schoolhouse.

The original church at Itchen Stoke, in a low-lying meadow near the river, was condemned as cold and damp. It was replaced, early last century, by a church on much higher ground but this also proved unsatisfactory for the same reason. After three decades or so it was demolished, to be supplanted in 1866 by the present building. Modelled on a chapel in Paris, this Church of St. Mary was built almost entirely at the expense of the Vicar, the Rev. Charles Ranken Conybeare, who employed his brother Henry as architect. The result is as eccentric a structure as adorns any

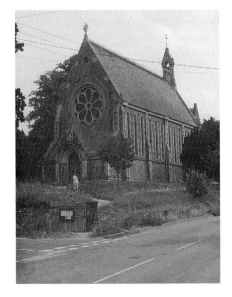

Itchen Stoke church

village in Hampshire, its exceptional loftiness accentuated by the hillock on which it stands. Twelve tall, lancet-shaped, stained glass windows are ranged along each side of the nave, which is integral with the chancel. Closed in 1971, the building is now looked after by the Fund for Redundant Churches, with just two services each year.

Walk 12 — A

Distance: Allow a generous hour for this one-and-a-half-mile stroll.

Overhanging trees shade the gravel path which leads you north from the quiet lane directly east of The Bush Inn to a wooden footbridge across the main arm of the Itchen. When I passed this way the wide and muddy-bottomed channel was populated by swans and sooty cygnets, white-pated coots, slightly smaller moorhens and not-so-wild duck, well used to the passage of pedestrians beside their sanctuary. Trout are easily spotted in the shallows of the willow-bordered sidestream to your right as your path bends left after crossing the principal channel.

With flowing water on both sides and luxuriant vegetation reaching out to brush your knees, you now wend westward to where the path is screened by trees from the main river. A little way farther on the walking route turns right to cross the sidestream on that side by a well-built concrete, wooden-railed footbridge. A seat on your left-hand side, just across this, is ideal for river-watching at a spot where there was once an important ford.

Many riverside strollers go no farther, but you continue along what becomes a tree-shaded by-way, Water Lane. A timber-framed cottage on your left precedes one of flint with a lovely garden as you now arrive at Itchen Stoke. At a point where

à la carte restaurant, seating 20, has an overflow area for busy times, and opens from 1100 to 1430 and 1800 to 2300, Mondays to Saturdays and from 1200 to 1500 and 1900 to 2230 on Sundays.

Traditional old world bric-a-brac on show includes a large bellows once used by the blacksmith at Ovington forge, which adjoined a cottage to the rear of the pub. A pleasant, tree-shaded garden has one of the shallower arms of the Itchen as its neighbour. The large car park, behind the pub, is available to walkers who intend to use the pub. Children are allowed into the lower bar except when the restaurant is full.

One of the bars is said to be haunted, the ghost expressing itself as 'a chilly presence', usually late in the evening after closing. Upstairs rooms with four-poster beds were once an advertised attraction until an enthusiastic honeymoon couple caused one of the beds to crash through into the bar below.

the village green spreads to your left and the flint-walled former school-house lies to your right your lane joins the King's Worthy-Alresford road. Turn right here and cross the road to visit the church, as thoroughly at odds with village architecture in general, and that of Itchen Stoke in particular, as could possibly be imagined. It is normally opened by a local lady who keeps the key, and a booklet on sale inside outlines its history and that of the village.

Recross the road to carry on east along the paved footway along its south side. Beyond the last house in the village a timbered park spreads down to the Itchen, faced by a public seat placed 'In memory of Arthur Terrill'. For several minutes I sat here to savour a scene in which somnolent cattle in rich summer greensward helped set the seal on rural enchantment of an ageless quality.

Where the macadamised footway ends a narrow, tree-lined lane turns right and leads you south to a narrow ford across one of the Itchen's several sidestreams. Motorists unmindful of risks to their suspension can treat their cars to a free wash by driving through at speed, but for walkers there is a footbridge. Beyond the ford your lane crosses a culvert and twists left past Ovington Mill, with its weedy mill-stream which joins the Itchen's main arm just below where you now cross it. You now join another narrow lane which you follow right-handed back to The Bush Inn, pausing en route to check the small sidestream to your left for lurking trout. Sycamores and beeches on a steep slope overhang this waterway and scenically embellish the last stage of this short walk.

Walk 12 — B

Distance: Allow 2-3 hours for this 4-mile walk.

A drowsy mallard duck was clearly resentful at being disturbed by me and my companion as we set off in morning sunshine to explore this longer route, which combines river valley footpaths with field-border and woodland tracks over the chalk country south-west of Ovington. As with Walk 12-A, you begin from The Bush Inn by following the gravel path north through riverside trees and over the mainstream of the Itchen, then turning left to head west between the main river and one of its sidestreams — the classic walk from Ovington.

Where the path turns right to bridge the sidestream you turn with it and carry on north along Water Lane into Itchen Stoke, where we turned aside to pay what was, for me, a second visit to the church. We found the door locked, but just at that moment the keyholder came to our rescue. Morning

Ovington to Itchen Stoke path

sunlight filtered through the impressive stained glass windows to illuminate a lofty nave and chancel, all of a piece with no screen between them. Memorials to parishioners long deceased tell many a story, and those in this 19th century church are no exception, One that especially caught my eye was dedicated to Annie, wife of the Henry Conybeare whom I presume to have been the architect who designed this building when his brother was the Vicar. A further pathetic dedication is to 10-year-old Mary, presumably their daughter, who died in 1861. Her decease inspired a couplet whose sentiments surely echo the grief of parents everywhere, in any age, who suddenly lose a child: 'Oh for the touch of a vanished hand and the sound of a voice that is still'.

Out again into the sunshine, we recrossed the main village road and headed west past the thatched and timber-framed cottages which flank it for the short distance to the far end of Itchen Stoke. Turn left here by a footpath sign, with a thatched cottage to your left, along a drive from which you fork right to follow a green track to a gate and two stiles leading into a meadow.

To your left here two former farm buildings constructed of brick, timber and flints have been converted into dwellings: quite common nowadays and much preferred to allowing picturesque old barns to fall to pieces.

The course of your footpath is briefly ill-defined as it leads across a pasture towards a gap between two ash trees where a footbridge spans a brook. A well-defined path continues across a meadow bestrewn in summer with flowers to a concrete footbridge with wooden handrails across the main body of the Itchen. The public footway here bends right and then left, with private riverside paths for fishermen branching off in both directions.

Trees shade your way to a further footbridge over a gravel-bottomed trout stream shaded in turn by bordering greenery. Roofed over by hedgerow timber, your path leads on along a hollow track away from the watery world

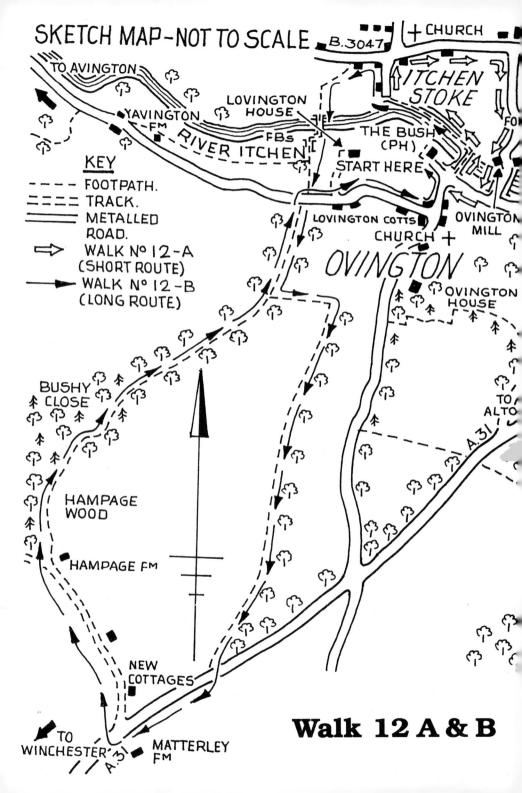

that has been your walk's setting up to this point. Disregard a right-turning public footpath as you head south to reach and cross the lane that links Avington with Ovington.

A tree-tunnelled bridleway leads ahead, beginning a steady climb into the chalk. At the end of the first field on your left look out for a footpath sign on your left, indicating a path which heads east along the south side of a hedgerow. The Pathfinder map suggests this should be on the other side of the hedge, indeed a stile, half-hidden by herbage, survives to support this supposition, but it seems this right of way has been changed at some time recently.

Anyway, follow this path to the far, eastern side of the field you now enter and there turn right to climb south-southwestward with, to your left, a broad belt of timber of a type sometimes labelled 'Hampshire hedgerow'. There are indeed many such in the county, more especially in chalky areas, substantially wider than normal hedgerows yet not wide enough to rank as woodlands. They provide welcome windbreaks and game coverts as well as enhancing the countryside scene. See how many trees species you can identify in this one: I recognised spindle, dogwood, sycamore, field maple, hawthorn, wayfaring tree and elder, among others.

Arable farmland to your right and hedgerow timber to your left border the broad green path you now follow for a mile. Traffic noise grows more insistent as you approach the A31, and when you reach this you follow its grassy right-hand verge in a right-hand direction. Within a few hundred yards, opposite Matterley Farm, turn right to follow a macadamised private farm road which is also a public bridleway — the sign 'no cars' appears twice alongside it. Beyond farm cottages and some modern style farm buildings on your right you pass Hampage Farm, where the tarmac ends.

Watch out now for a three-way bridleway sign, at which point you turn right to follow a tributary bridleway heading north-east into Hampage Wood. Today a mixture of dark conifers and broadleaved trees of no great age, this wood is famous for the story concerning it about Bishop Walkelyn of Winchester having persuaded the King to allow him as much timber as could be felled in one night as roofing material for his cathedral. By morning an army of workmen had cut down every worthwhile tree.

Your narrow path heads north between the wood edge, not many yards to your right, and a green ride dimly visible through plantations to your left. Leaving the wood, your path tunnels on through hedgerow timber to bring you back on to the Avington-Ovington lane. Follow this right, past Lovington Cottages — Lovington House lies to your left here — to a T-junction where you turn left and head downhill past Ovington's cottages back to The Bush Inn and your car.

River and Down near Alresford

WALK 13

Allow **4 hours**

6 miles

Walk begins page 88

Background to the Walk

Not many towns or villages have as clearly defined an origin as New Alresford, in the heart of Hampshire. For reasons never clearly explained, the original Alresford — Old Alresford — was not thought a suitable location for expansion into the market town Winchester Bishop Godfrey de Lucy wanted. Around 1200 he therefore laid plans for a new community to the south of the headstream of the Itchen known as the Alre.

The shape of the town he planned is the same today in its basic essentials, with modern development around the fringes as the only significant difference. Its most distinctive feature, Broad Street, survives to remind us of the importance attached by the Bishop to having an area of suitable size for sheep fairs and other such gatherings.

At much the same time, the River Alre was dammed to create Old Alresford Pond. Why this was done has been much debated, the most popular theory being that it was made to provide an adequate head of water for making the Itchen navigable this far upstream. Linked with the Bishop's grand design for local development, this might seem likely. Local historians, however, now hold the view that the pond was created for purely episcopal convenience, to stock fish for use when the prelate was in residence at the palace at Bishop's Sutton.

As for the 'River Alre' itself, it has been sug-

Maps
Landranger 1:50,000
Sheet 185
Pathfinder 1:25,000
Sheet SU 43/53
Map Reference of
Start/Finish SU588325

How to get there
From Southampton follow A33 and M3 to Winchester bypass. Half a mile beyond Hockley traffic lights filter left to follow A31 to the roundabout at the start of Alresford bypass, from which you follow B3047 on into New Alresford. Turn right at the top of West Street to reach the car park by the station. Solent Blue bus service 47 connects at Winchester on weekdays only with Hampshire Bus service 67 to Petersfield via New Alresford, and with Alder Valley buses on services 214 and 215, terminating either at Old Alresford or continuing to Guild-

gested that the name is wholly unwarranted for what should rightly be regarded as the main headstream of the Itchen, and ought to be designated accordingly. This school of thought maintains that the longer, alternative headwater, which rises above Cheriton, should cease to be called the Itchen and merely be known as the Tichborne stream. Whatever the rights and wrongs of this argument, the unpronounceable name 'Alre' is commonly modified to 'Arle', the name of the town being modified still further to sound like 'Awlsfud' — it derives from the Old English for 'alder-tree ford'.

New Alresford's urban continuity was punctuated at intervals over the centuries by fire. At least one was started deliberately, by retreating Royalists out of spite at its inhabitants' Roundhead sympathies, after the King's men were routed at Cheriton in 1644. In 1689 another fire severely damaged the Church of St. John the Baptist, which had been rebuilt by Bishop de Lucy on the site of a predecessor recorded in Domesday. The present church dates from 1898 and retains few fragments from earlier times. In the churchyard are the graves of French prisoners of war who died while working in the town during Napoleonic times.

One of New Alresford's most famous residents was Admiral Lord Rodney, whose 18th century triumphs against the fleets of France and Spain assured him a place in our naval history equal almost to that of Nelson. Mary Russell Mitford's birthplace in Broad Street bears a plaque recording this detail in the life of the author of *Our Village*, *Country Sketches* and of sundry plays and poems which few nowadays remember. A distinguished townsperson of more recent vintage was cricket commentator and writer John Arlott, who lived for much of his life in East Street, at The Old Sun, a former pub. If reports of the depth and quality of his wine cellar are true then certainly

ford after passing through New Alresford. On Sundays Oakley Coaches operate service 453 from Winchester to Aldershot via New Alresford.

Pub facilities

The Swan Hotel, *the town's main inn for more than two centuries was once a staging point for coaches between Southampton and London. The hotel caters for modern needs and has two large car parks for customers. Restaurant facilities, recently extended, include the historic undercroft, which seats 120. Bar food ranges from soups and sandwiches to three-course Sunday lunches The bar is open from 1100-2300 weekdays (usual times on Sundays). Courage ales, Guinness and cider available. Food is served from 1200-1430 and 1900-2300, children's dishes available.*

Opposite is **The Bell Hotel**, *once known as The Market Inn. An alehouse probably existed on the site in the 16th century. At a later stage of its history a highwayman hung* *himself in one of the seven bedrooms. A stable block at the back survives from when horse-drawn coaches conveyed the hostelry's customers. Normal pub hours and facilities include a choice of real ales such as HSB, Webster's and Watney's Bitter, as well as draught Guinness and cider. Bar snacks and à la carte restaurant service are available. The hotel caters for groups of ramblers by prior arrangement. Well-behaved dogs acceptable.*

The Peaceful Home *in East Street lives up to its name as a free house with traditional pub facilities including Ringwood Bitter and Bass from hand pumps, Worthington Best Bitter, Worthington Dark (mild), Murphy's stout, draught cider, plus a choice of hot and cold snacks. There is also restaurant service in summer and you can book here for bed and breakfast. There are facilities for children and a small beer garden. Opening hours at this centuries old pub in a grade II listed building, are 1100-1400 and 1800-2300*

the 'house' was much better stocked when it was private than when it was public! Also on a literary theme but back in Broad Street (No.17) don't miss the opportunity of visiting Laurence Oxley, the antiquarian and secondhand bookshop.

New Alresford's charm as an old country town is matched in appeal for many visitors by its being headquarters of the Mid-Hants Railway or Watercress Line. The original Alton-Winchester railway formed part of an alternative route to the main line via Basingstoke for London-Southampton trains. Closed in 1973, it has been progressively reopened as a steam train enthusiasts' haven apart from the Alresford-Winchester section, which has faded into history, seemingly never to return. The name recalls times when this local product was despatched by train in quantities to customers in London and elsewhere. It is still extensively grown but reaches the markets by other means now.

Once a sizeable village with a mill on Candover Stream, another headstream of the Itchen, Abbotstone is now merely a farmhouse and a cottage or two at an intersection of lanes which hardly anyone but locals traverse.

Walk 13

Distance: Allow up to 4 hours for this 6-mile walk.

Parking space in Alresford is in short supply these days so we parked by the station. From just across the road a footpath leads through the yewy churchyard, past the Church of St. John the Baptist. Almost completely rebuilt three years before Queen Victoria died, it retains little of its past apart from a tower from the 14th century topped with brick 300 years later.

Leaving the churchyard by the main entrance, cross the main road and head down Broad Street, with its variegated rooflines and assorted architectural styles harmoniously interwoven. For a

The old fulling mill, Alresford

peep at Old Alresford Pond turn right at the bottom into The Soke. This last name has nothing to do with wetness despite the proximity of water but dates from times when land thus designated was under the jurisdiction of a manorial court of law.

Return to the bottom of Broad Street to follow Mill Hill, which continues north from it, then turn left along Ladywell Lane to follow a section of the long distance Wayfarer's Walk (from Emsworth in south-east Hampshire to Inkpen Beacon, Berkshire). A metalled path diverges right from this, with a stream on your right-hand side, and Alresford's War Memorial Park, with its thatched lych-gate, is passed a little way along on your left. Your path becomes gravelled as it leads on past the most photographed secular building hereabouts: a thatched, whitewashed and timber-framed 13th century former fulling mill, picturesquely straddling the River Alre and well preserved as a private residence. Re-thatching was under way when we passed. On its exterior is a notice hinting at punitive retribution against 'all persons found Fishing in these waters (without special leave given for the occasion by the owner of the Fishery)'. The appended date, 1853, may add a colourful

Monday to Friday, all day Saturday and as usual on Sunday.
In Broad Street, **The Horse and Groom** opens weekdays between 1100-1430 and 1800-2300, and at the usual times on Sundays. It preserves much evidence of the times when equestrian traffic gave special relevance to its name. The bar menu includes such local specialities as Alresford trout with almonds, home made steak and kidney pie and much else. Real ales include Fremlin's, Boddington's, Strong Country and Marston's Pedigree. Food can be ordered between 1200-1400 (1415 on Sundays) and 1800-2100 (2200 on Fridays and Saturdays).
Round the corner on your right from the bottom of Broad Street, in The Soke, is **The Globe Inn**, open from 1100-2300 weekdays (Sundays as usual) and with traditional Hampshire HSB, Ruddle's and Webster's real ales on tap. Bar food between 1200 and 1400 and from 1900-2200. It has a large rear window ideal for birdwatchers studying Old Alresford

Pond, on to which the rear garden abuts. Mallard, teal, tufted duck, pochard and Canada geese were to be seen when I last called. The pond and its immediate surrounds are private property, a footpath which once led past it to Bishop's Sutton having been closed. The pond, once three times as large, is retained by the Great Weir, a mediaeval earthwork along which runs the Basingstoke road.

period flavour but I have little doubt that the warning is no less applicable now.

The gravel riverside path winds on to the lower end of a cul-de-sac called The Dean. Head half-right here to continue along a firm path through trees by the river, presently crossing a subsidiary brook by a semi-derelict brick building. After a further short distance your footpath crosses the River Alre proper by a culvert. Joining another path, hedged on your left and with arable farmland to your right, you now head west to join a lane with which you converge from the left.

The lane leads ahead for a few yards to where you cross it to follow a hedged, right-turning gravel road signposted as a 'right of way'. A little way along this we passed a cluster of caravans parked illegally, out of sight of the metalled road. A mile farther on we passed more caravans. If you have a similar encounter on this or any other walk, report the facts to Hampshire County Council, who will then take appropriate action.

Gravel gives way to grass as you continue along this byway to its junction with a tree-hedged stony lane, which you follow left-handed. After bridging the Candover Stream this lane heads pleasantly west, uphill, to give right-hand views across the placid Candover Valley towards Abbotstone. After crossing a narrow metalled lane carry on, north-west now, climbing still, between scrub hedgerows, to the meeting point of five green lanes near the top of Itchen Stoke Down, where we found a sheltered corner to enjoy our sandwiches in the sunshine.

Now follow another scrub-hedged green lane, turning sharp right from the one last followed and signposted as a walking route to Abbotstone and Farnham. If Farnham is a day's march away, Abbotstone is pleasingly close now and it is downhill all the way there. Where two metalled lanes converge at the foot of a half-mile descent keep straight to pass the first of Abbotstone's few dwellings on your left. Cross the rippling Candover Stream and then continue ahead uphill, with leftward views across a valley farmhouse and its outbuildings to the timbered southern extremity of The Grange Park, Northington.

Where the metalled lane bends right here, carry on left-ahead along a fenced green lane. This soon veers right and is bordered by scrub hedgerows which give way in turn to a clipped hedge. Scrub hedgerows

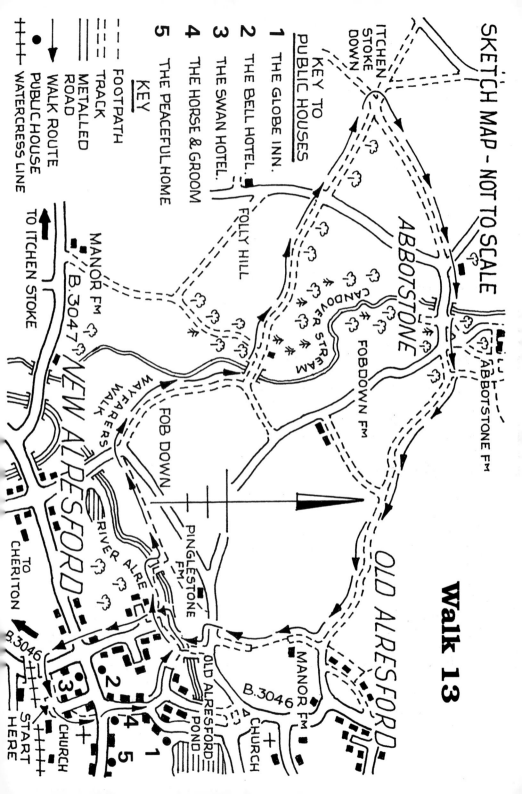

SKETCH MAP - NOT TO SCALE

Walk 13

KEY TO PUBLIC HOUSES

1 THE GLOBE INN.
2 THE BELL HOTEL.
3 THE SWAN HOTEL.
4 THE HORSE & GROOM
5 THE PEACEFUL HOME

KEY

— — — FOOTPATH
= = = TRACK
——— METALLED ROAD
→ WALK ROUTE
● PUBLIC HOUSE
+++ WATERCRESS LINE

ITCHEN STOKE DOWN
ABBOTSTONE
ABBOTSTONE FM
CANDOVER STREAM
FOBDOWN FM
FOLLY HILL
MANOR FM
B.3047
NEW ALRESFORD
TO ITCHEN STOKE
WAYFARERS WALK
FOB DOWN
RIVER ALRE
PINGLESTONE FM.
OLD ALRESFORD
MANOR FM.
B.3046
OLD ALRESFORD POND
CHURCH
TO CHERITON
B.3046
CHURCH
START HERE

Tree-shaded byway

then resume, with right-hand views towards Fob Down Farm, from which a farm road climbs to join your own as you carry on south-east.

At the approaches to Old Alresford your green lane joins a public road. Here you turn right past Manor Farm and a thatched, weatherboarded barn, with left-hand views of Old Alresford church across an intervening valley. Beyond the farm you follow another green lane as far as a private notice, at which point you cross a stile or pass through a hedge-gap on your right to follow a path along the leftward edge of an arable field. At this field's end cross a stile and angle right to follow a path in front of the garden of a house, joining a gravel drive which then leads you out on to a metalled motor road. Follow this leftward to where a driveway with a bridleway sign at its start leads you right-handed beside a tributary rivulet of the Alre, emerging through trees to bridge the River Alre itself by the old fulling mill you passed soon after you started.

Follow the riverside path right-handed to the bottom end of The Dean, which leads you south past Victorian terraces and industrial premises to reach the lower end of West Street and the town centre of New Alresford. The Old School House Restaurant, to your left here, occupies premises which until 1932 housed a grammar school founded in 1697 by a Dr. Henry Perin and still known locally as Perin's Grammar School.

Cross the main road and head south towards the railway bridge now in front of you before turning left to follow a signposted metalled footpath to Station Road, which you follow right-handed back to the car park.

A Chalk Walk from Cheriton

WALK 14

Allow **3 hours**

5 miles

Walk begins page 95

Background to the Walk

Despite the pressures of modern traffic, Cheriton is one of those villages which preserve something of the timeless rural calm of earlier times. This is exemplified by the tranquil village green, surrounded by cottages no two of which are alike, bisected by the crystal-clear channel of an infant River Itchen and haunted by numerous duck which maintain a beady-eyed alertness for possible handouts from passers-by. Yes, here is village peace of the kind townspeople idealise. Yet there are reminders of things less peaceful. At one corner of the green is a simple village war memorial. Headed '1914-1919. For England', it lists the names of 13 Cheriton men, imbued with the patriotic spirit which sustained so many then, who left their homes in Hampshire's countryside to set off for the heat of battle, never to return. It also names the half-dozen who made the same supreme sacrifice between 1939 and 1945. Also included are verses of that sad and lovely hymn I can recall from pre-World War II Armistice Day church services attended as a schoolboy :
'O valiant hearts who to your glory came
Through dust of conflict and through battle flame
Tranquil you lie, your knightly virtue proved
Your memory hallowed in the land you loved.'
As if this were not reminder enough of just how fragile peace is apt to be, a mile to the east of Cheriton, a cross-swords symbol on the map denotes a civil war battle in which Crown and

Maps
Landranger 1:50,000
Sheet 185
Pathfinder 1:25,000
Sheet SU 42/52
Map Reference of
Start/Finish SU582283

How to get there
From Southampton follow A33 and M3 to Winchester bypass and leave at the first interchange beyond Hockley traffic lights to follow A31 and then A272 to Petersfield. At first crossroads on A272 turn left to Cheriton, just after entering which you will see The Flower Pots on the right. Or carry on to join and follow B3046 left for a few yards and park by the village green, to your right. Solent service 47 from Southampton connects at Winchester with Hampshire Bus service 67 between Winchester and Petersfield, passing through Cheriton.

Pub facilities
The Flower Pots

(pictured right) was once the home of a retired estate head gardener whose three-acre smallholding is still part of the property and is available for use in summer by campers and caravanners. Log fires lend old-fashioned comfort to both bars, where Hop Back Summer Lightning from Salisbury and Ringwood Best were among real ales available when I called. You can choose from a range of hot bar food, cold snacks and sandwiches. Typical items on the menu range from beef stew and no less warming chilli con carne — with or without crusty bread or garlic bread — to ever more popular jacket potatoes. There is a children's room. Well-behaved dogs are admitted to this very friendly free house and walkers intending to be pub customers are welcome to use the pub car park. Opening times are 1100-1430 and 1800-2300 on weekdays and the usual pub hours (1200-1500 and 1900-2230) on Sundays.

Commonwealth confronted each other and wreaked great slaughter. Cromwell's men prevailed, their victory marking the beginning of the end for the Royalist cause. On a bright spring day in 1644, these fighting men had no need to seek some corner of a foreign field on which to lay down their lives for a cause, though whether any Cheriton men succumbed is not recorded. The grave-mounds of some of the 2,000 fallen may still be seen along one local laneside. Members of the English Civil War Society re-enact the Battle of Cheriton here on appropriate occasions. A stone memorial alongside the lane that leads from Cheriton to Ropley commemorates the original encounter.

Cheriton pre-dates recorded history. Its Church of St. Michael and All Angels was built in the 12th century by Bishop Henry de Blois of Winchester on a prehistoric long barrow, and the name of the Itchenside community means simply 'the homestead by the church'. In Saxon times there were links with nearby Tichborne, and villagers are still among beneficiaries of the 'Tichborne Dole', an annual distribution of flour carried out in observance of a centuries-old charity. Watercress-growing and truffle-hunting survived locally until the present century and Cheriton's isolation ended in

1925 with the arrival of the first buses.

Until 1961 there were three pubs in the village. First to go was The Bricklayers Arms, to be followed in 1986 by the H. H. Inn, which I used occasionally. Both are now private dwellings. The H. H. Inn recalled the one-time presence at Cheriton of the kennels of that hunt.

Walk 14

Distance: Allow up to 3 hours for this 5-mile walk.

From The Flower Pots follow the road on into Cheriton village centre, with the timbered and flint-walled grounds of Cheriton Old Rectory to your left as a reminder of the style in which country clerics used to live. Many were the younger sons of well-to-do landed families and so were accustomed to the best.

Joining B3046, follow this left-handed past the village green with its board-banked rivulet, its predatory ducks and its war memorial. The Itchen enters and leaves the green by way of brick culverts bearing the warning words 'Take notice: this bridge is insufficient to carry weights beyond ordinary traffic. By order. James Symes, District Surveyor'. When James Symes held sway I do not know, but perhaps his warning was meant for drivers of those steam-driven traction engines which lumbered about our country byways in the early years of this century.

The 12th century church on its elevated long barrow foundation lies back to your left, opposite the green. It was locked when I did this walk, with no indication as to who might hold the key. Also to your left as you carry on past the green is the brick-and-pebbledash parish hall built in 1911.

Having passed the former H. H. Inn and a thatched cottage just beyond, turn left to follow Hill Houses Lane. This rises between high banks where the bushes in winter are draped with old man's beard, as the grey and whiskery clematis which produces this growth is popularly called. Soon reached is the thatch-and-flint hamlet of Hill Houses, where you fork right to follow an unmetalled private road which is also a public bridleway. Hedged pastures rise to your right as the bridleway leads you westward, over a ridge and then on down into a vale towards a barn which lies left-ahead.

On the near side of the barn I found a barbed-wire 'gate' stretched taut across the entrance to the green lane turning left, which I next meant to follow. This turned out to be a temporary deterrent to straying by cattle being driven along the bridleway to new pastures, although there was

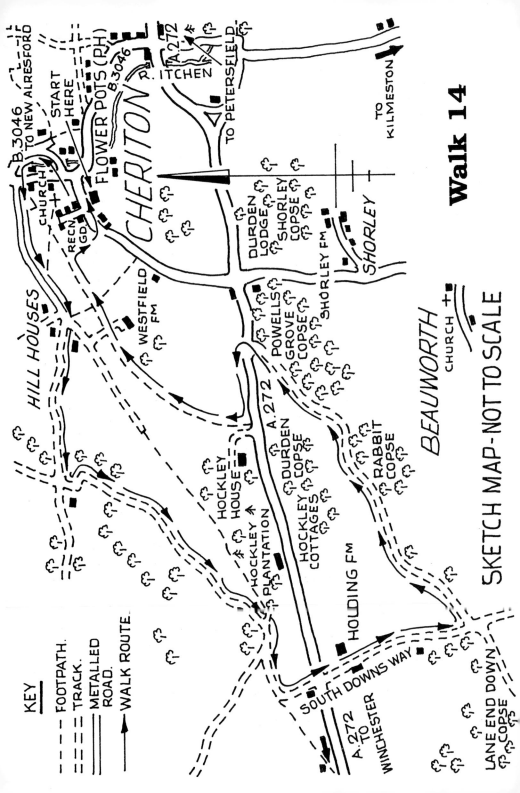

Walk 14

SKETCH MAP - NOT TO SCALE

KEY
- - - - FOOTPATH.
= = = = TRACK.
―――― METALLED ROAD.
→ WALK ROUTE.

B.3046 TO NEW ALRESFORD
START HERE
FLOWER POTS (PH)
B.3046
CHURCH.
RECN. GD.
CHERITON
ITCHEN
A.272
TO PETERSFIELD
TO KILMESTON
A.272

HILL HOUSES
WESTFIELD FM
DURDEN LODGE
SHORLEY COPSE
SHORLEY FM
SHORLEY

POWELL'S GROVE COPSE
DURDEN COPSE
HOCKLEY HOUSE
HOCKLEY PLANTATION
HOCKLEY COTTAGES
RABBIT COPSE
HOLDING FM
BEAUWORTH
CHURCH +

SOUTH DOWNS WAY
A.272 TO WINCHESTER
LANE END DOWN COPSE

nothing to indicate this until the farmer arrived with his charges after I had reached this point. Such 'gates' across public rights of way are illegal as permanent fixtures.

Following a gently rising dry vale deep in chalk country, the green lane leads you south-westward into a lonely, peaceful region where you can almost forget that such things as the noise pollution of motor traffic and the multiform pressures of ever increasing human multitudes ever existed. It needs but the song of a soaring skylark or the plaintive cry of a peewit to round off a setting of sheer enchantment.

South Downs Way crossing the A272 near Holdings Farm, near Cheriton

Scattered oaks merge into wayside groves of denser timber before your green lane joins another, which you follow to the right. The well-defined trackway ends at a metal gate flanked by a stile, beyond which your right of way follows the leftward margin of a downland cattle pasture for a short distance. Another metal gate to your left precedes a section of the recently extended South Downs Way, now available as a walking route from Winchester to the eastern extremity of the downs, at Beachy Head. Following it for a little way, a green track bordered by trees leads you downhill to the A272, which you cross to follow a hard-surfaced farm road past Holdings Farm and its outbuildings.

Beyond these you follow a beech-bordered 'dirt' road for nearly half a mile to a crossing of tracks in a vale. Turn left here to follow a green track with a tall hedge to your right and with arable farmland rising to broadleaved woodland on your left. Balls Lane, as this track is called, descends north-eastward past Rabbit Copse where I saw my first wild rabbit on this walk. Decimated in the mid-'fifties by myxomatosis, rabbits are no longer rare through they still have quite a long way to go to recover their pre-epidemic numbers (farmers and foresters hope that this may never happen).

It was along here that I met an octogenarian farmer who could recall, he said, driving a pony-trap along Balls Lane to church services in the old school at Lane End, a chalkland hamlet on the Warnford-Winchester road, not far away. In his young days the smallest villages and hamlets all had schools, but nowadays local children are bussed to Cheriton or Alresford for their education. Offered a lift in his four-wheel-drive farm vehicle, I thanked him and opted to carry on walking in the interests of this book. In the process I had to circumvent pond-size puddles along the section of

Farm lane west of Hill Houses, Cheriton

Balls Lane that is flanked on the right by Powells Grove Copse before it emerges on to A272.

Watch out for fast traffic zooming round the bends as you follow the main road sharp left for a few hundred yards. Just short of where a driveway turns right for Hockley House Stud, a footpath sign points your way right-handed along the leftward edge of a field. Reaching a tree hedge at the far end of this, I had to probe through bushes to find and cross a stile preceding a pasture. Following the leftward edge of the latter, I surprised a solitary roe deer which went bounding away right-handed alongside the hedge at the end of the pasture. After crossing another stile here, ignore a stile on your left and follow the left edge of the next pasture to a further stile.

Beyond this you descend a bank to cross a farm road and negotiate what I found to be a bushed-in, broken-stepped stile (I did my best to subdue the most obstructive vegetation). The leftward edge of the next field precedes a final stile leading into Cheriton Recreation Ground, where the footpath proper continues behind the changing rooms but proved to be so hopelessly overgrown when I arrived here that I turned right to reach the road by way of the recreation ground. I suggest you do likewise. Follow the road for a very short distance left-handed back into the village, where The Flower Pots looms invitingly to your right.

Hedged Pastures near Durley and Bishop's Waltham

WALK 15

Up to **3 hours**

5 miles

Walk begins page 100

Background to the Walk

Nearly all of southern Hampshire was at one time heavily wooded. The Forest of Bere, now small and fragmented, originally spread right across the region to form a continuous belt of wild ground virtually linking up with The New Forest. Durley began as a farming settlement in a forest clearing to which wild animals would have had access, hence perhaps its name, which may be interpreted as 'deer meadow'. There are deer in local woods today. They sometimes stray into the meadows, and more than once I have seen them on open farmland near where this walk starts.

Durley developed not as a compact village but as a scattering of farms with their associated cottages. So it largely remains today, with the addition of many non-agricultural dwellings from the 19th century and later. The little church, where naturalist-cleric Gilbert White once preached, lies near the western fringe of the parish, remote from most of its inhabitants, while the Robin Hood pub lies at the other end, on the brink of a broad green vale beyond which the Hampshire chalk begins.

Lying as it does in the Hampshire Basin, Durley's countryside is predominantly grass farmland rather than arable. Still well-hedged in the 1990s, this farmland is crisscrossed by numerous footpaths connecting disparate parts of the parish and segmented by pretty, winding lanes whose inadequate surfacing, in times past, gave rise to

Maps
Landranger 1:50,000
Sheet 196
Pathfinder 1:25,000
Sheet SU 41/51
Map Reference of
Start/Finish SU528178

How to get there
From Southampton follow A3024 and A334 past Bitterne, through Thornhill and over M27 to a roundabout where you turn left to follow Tollbar Way (B3342), crossing B3035 and continuing ahead to B3354 which you cross and keep straight on through Durley, towards the far end of which, at Durley Street, the Robin Hood pub lies to your right. Apart from the pub car park there is limited parking space just short of it, on the right by a telephone kiosk. Solent Blue buses on services 48C (Eastleigh-Swanmore), X48 (Southampton-Eastleigh-Swanmore-

Waltham Chase) and
52 (Southampton-
Petersfield) pass this
point.

**Pub facilities
The Robin Hood.**
A Marston's pub open
on weekdays from
1100-1430 (1500 on
Saturdays) and from
1800-2300, Sunday
opening hours being as
usual. No facilities for
children but well-
behaved dogs are
acceptable. No food is
available at this village
'local' but walkers
using the pub may use
the pub car park.

the epithet 'dirty' Durley — today undeserved and
all but forgotten, so perhaps I should not have
resurrected it!

The Robin Hood is a village pub of the old-
fashioned sort where local people tend to outnum-
ber visitors. Engage them in conversation if you want to learn a little about
the Durley of yesteryear. One man I spoke to recalled the period, ending
in 1932, when the little branch railway between Botley and Bishop's
Waltham was still fully functional. His leisure time routine then was to
walk across the fields to Durley Halt, tucked away out of sight behind
Durley Mill on the River Hamble, and take a penny train ride from there
to line's end at Bishop's Waltham where, on arrival at the station, a penny
inserted in a slot machine produced a bar of chocolate. The homeward
journey, after such extravagance, was necessarily done on foot.

Walk 15

Distance: A trifle under 5 miles; allow 3 hours for leisurely walking.

With the Robin Hood just behind you, turn right at the hilltop crossroads
to follow Manor Road, bordered by dwellings which mostly date from late
Victorian times or the early years of the present century. This was a period
when the population of Durley grew considerably. The chief claim to fame
by Durley Manor is that two sisters of Oliver Cromwell are supposed to
have spent some time there. Durley Manor Farm lies a few hundred yards
beyond where you turn left from Manor Road after following it to where

houses on your left give way to farmland. Your path here begins by taking you through what looks like a private yard between the last house and an outbuilding. It leads on past a pony paddock to a robust wooden stile beyond which a well-defined right of way follows the left side of the paddock, with a shallow wooded gully to your left.

Tree-hedged valley fields ahead of you make a pleasing panorama as you cross a second stile, beyond which a meadow dips right-handed in front of you, with a small wood to the right of it. Your route now leads right-ahead, cutting directly across the meadow and steering slightly left of the wood to reach a stile on the far side, preceding the weathered remains of an elongated earthwork topped by trees. This stretches right-handed for a mile or more to the Hamble River valley. Known as the Park Lug, it marks the boundary of a park that was once an extensive pleasure ground attached to Bishop's Waltham Palace, the Bishops of Winchester's country retreat from mediaeval times.

You now head diagonally right across a downward-sloping field and over a dilapidated iron gate at its far corner. Continue ahead in a straight line across the next pasture to a stile which you cross, then keep straight on to cross another stile just to the right of a brick stream culvert. Here you emerge on to Tangier Lane, with Tangier Farmhouse and its outbuildings overlooking you from your right. Follow hedged Tangier Lane left-handed, gently uphill through pleasant countryside. Suddenly this changes as you reach the outer edges of modern development which has spread out from Bishop's Waltham in several directions. The dwellings concerned are pleasant enough, but they add nothing to the visual appeal of an ancient town.

Continue ahead along the suburbanised northern end of Tangier Lane to reach the main Bishop's Waltham—Winchester road, B2177, which you cross and follow right-handed. After a very few yards turn left to follow a road called Battery Hill, which also serves an estate of fairly new houses. This soon joins another road, which you cross to follow a concreted track left-ahead, uphill, to the right of dwellings. A gap in a fence leads into a diamond-shaped field across which you continue, veering away from the right-hand hedge as you cross high ground. Beyond the brow of the hill you head for a white-barred stile at the field's far corner, having crossed which you follow a well-defined path ahead along the right-hand edge of an oak-bordered pasture.

Keep straight on to cross three more stiles and emerge right-handed of farm buildings on to Ashton Lane, within yards of Park Dairy Farm. Cross the lane and follow it right-handed for a few steps before heading where a footpath sign on its west side points uphill. A driveway now leads you past

Walk 15

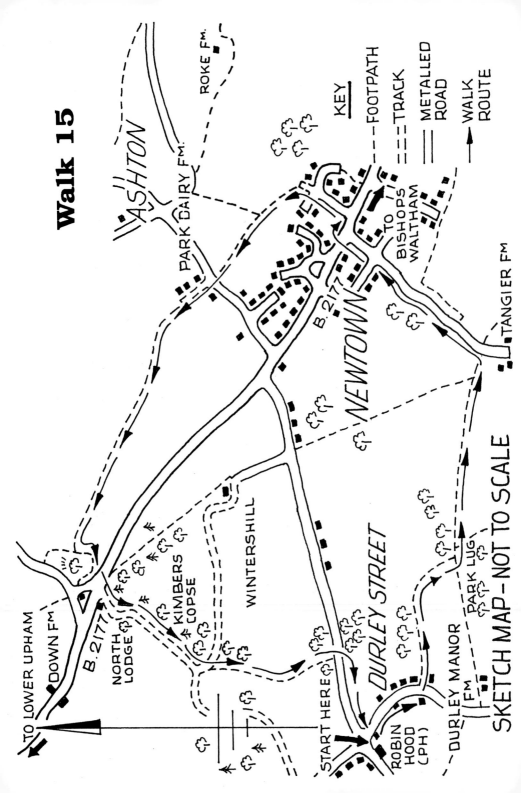

ASHTON

ROKE FM.

PARK DAIRY FM.

KEY
‑‑‑‑‑ FOOTPATH
‑ ‑ ‑ TRACK
═══ METALLED ROAD
→ WALK ROUTE

TO BISHOPS WALTHAM

B.2177

NEWTOWN

TANGIER FM.

B.2177

PARK LUG

DURLEY STREET

DURLEY MANOR FM.

ROBIN HOOD (PH)

START HERE

WINTERSHILL

KIMBERS COPSE

NORTH LODGE

B.2177

DOWN FM.

TO LOWER UPHAM

SKETCH MAP – NOT TO SCALE

Tangier Lane

a right-hand bungalow, then through a yard to the left of farm buildings to a metal gate preceding a horse paddock, parts of which I found had been churned into a mudbath.

Braving probable moist conditions, keep straight on along the left side of the paddock to cross a stile at its far side and reach what I found to be the first bit of arable farmland on this walk. This change is largely due to your having reached the foothills of the chalk.

An earth path leads straight on along the line of a former field boundary to the bend of an L-shaped hedge, with the base of the L heading to your left. Follow the leg of the L for a yard or so, then pass through a gap in the hedge to your left. Now follow the right-hand edge of the field you have just entered, cross a decrepit stile at the end of it and continue along the right-hand edge of the pasture beyond. A gap in the hedge at the end of this precedes a second pasture, through which you continue to a stile at its far right-hand corner.

Cross this and then turn left to follow the leftward edge of an area of weedy, semi-waste ground. Bend right where the fence and hedge to your left do the same, cross a stream by a wooden footbridge and bend right again to reach a stile preceding a narrow, tree-lined lane which you follow left-handed. Within a very short distance this brings you back on to the B2177, which you cross and follow right-handed for a few yards before turning left to follow a grass-and-gravel driveway, passing on your right the North Lodge of Wintershill estate.

Hedged on your right and bordered by a wood called Kimbers Copse on your left, this drive, a public footpath, leads to a T-junction of such tracks. Here the right of way turns left. Within yards a footpath sign points your way right-handed, through a metal gate and then by way of a fenced path along the length of a strip of woodland. A wooden fence gives way to barbed-wire, and where the latter ends in its turn go through a metal gate ahead to follow the right-hand edge of a meadow. At the end of this a stile precedes a tree-shaded final few yards to the Bishop's Waltham—Durley road. Cross this and follow the grass verge on its far side as you now head right-handed, uphill, for the last couple of hundred yards back to The Robin Hood.

A Meon Valley and Downland Walk from Droxford

WALK 16
4 to 5 hours
8 miles
Walk begins page 106

Background to the Walk

Located about halfway along the picturesque Meon Valley, Droxford has been a centre of population more or less continuously since the Jutish Meonwara settled hereabouts not long after the Romans left Britain. Its Church of St. Mary and All Saints is in part Norman though it has been embellished and restored in subsequent periods including, inevitably, that heyday of church 'restoration', the 19th century. The result is a chunky, solid structure of a size appropriate to the village it serves: a village notable for its wealth of Georgian dwellings crowding a main street woefully narrow and inadequate for the volume of traffic funnelled through it along the A32 in the absence of a bypass.

Yet where could any such bypass go without wholly unacceptable harm to the local environment — harm as scarring and unthinkable as any to have stirred the public conscience in recent times? On one side flows the Meon, the Hampshire chalk stream known so well by Izaak Walton. On the other side loom the downs, and any who might doubt the destructive impact a bypass would make on the local downland scene need only tackle the walk to convince themselves that the chalk country flanking Droxford is, beyond question, an area of outstanding natural beauty which needs no official designation.

Environmental considerations did not stand in the way of plans by the London and South Western

Maps
Landranger 1:50,000 Sheet 185 Pathfinder 1:25,000 Sheets SU 61/71, SU 41/51, SU 42/52 and SU 62/72 Map Reference of Start/ Finish SU607183

How to get there
From Southampton follow A3024, A334 and B3035 via Bitterne centre bypass, Thornhill and Botley to Bishop's Waltham roundabout. From this continue along B3035 towards Corhampton for a few hundred yards then take the second turning right, leading to a T-junction where you turn left for Swanmore. Carry on through Swanmore to the crossroads by The Hunters Inn and turn left there for Droxford, where you join and follow left-ahead A32. The White Horse and The Bakers Arms are both on the right of the village main street. At

Railway Company to thwart a scheme by their GWR rivals to build a line along the valley. The railway, linking Alton and Fareham, was opened in 1903 but never justified its cost. Passenger trains survived until 1955 when I travelled the length of the line just before its closure. When the railway was being constructed a Jutish cemetery was discovered at Droxford. Another claim to fame by the old Meon Valley line is the hospitality it gave to Churchill, Eisenhower and others who used a special train at Droxford station as their temporary headquarters at the time of the D-Day landings in Normandy in June, 1944. Part of the railway's route today is a public bridleway and footpath.

How did Droxford's name originate? The 'ford' part explains itself, but 'Drox', deriving from 'Drochene' and other earlier spellings, is puzzling, unless it stems from the Old English word 'drochen', meaning 'dry place'. In this case 'Droxford' must be a tautology. Less mysterious is nearby Exton, apparently a contraction of a 10th century name, East Seaxnatune, meaning 'farmstead of the East Saxons'. Corhampton, it seems, is a corruption of 'Cornhampton', meaning 'home farm or settlement where grain is produced' — or so says A. D. Mills in his *Dictionary of English Place-Names* (OUP). The same source interprets Meonstoke as 'outlying farmstead on the River Meon'.

Of these latter three villages, Exton is touched upon only briefly on this walk. Corhampton is best known for its pre-Norman church which has neither spire, tower nor any known dedication and is neighboured by a yew which is possibly older than itself. Domesday Book records two mill sites here, one still functioning in the early 20th century. Meonstoke's Church of St. Andrew retains some 13th century fabric. Its 15th century tower was repaired in 1900 and embellished with an open-sided canopy: a striking visual feature.

the foot of the hill between the two, on your right, are spaces for parking on the corner where a cul-de-sac leads to the church. Hampshire Bus service 52 between Southampton and Petersfield passes through Droxford.

Pub facilities
*Droxford's **White Horse Inn** is reckoned to be 500 years old. This bow-windowed free house has beamed ceilings, a well-appointed restaurant and family room. It is much visited by walkers, who may use the pub car park if they are using the pub. The home made pies are recommended. Pub opening times are 1100-1500 and 1800-2300 on weekdays and 1200-1500 and 1900-2230 on Sundays. Food orders between 1200-1400 and 1900-2145.*

Bakers Arms Hotel, *another old-established hostelry towards the other end of the village. Open from 1100-1500 and from 1800-2300 (1200-1500 and 1900-2230 on Sundays), The Bakers Arms takes orders for food between 1200-1400 and*

Droxford

1800-2130 seven days a week. The emphasis is on home cooking, beef stew and dumplings proving a great favourite on the late autumn day when I called. Ind Coope mild, Friary Meux and Burton draught beers on tap. Apricot, raspberry, peach and other country wines available. Pub users may use the car park. B&B accommodation for long distance walkers following The South Downs Way or The Wayfarer's Walk.

*En route is **The Buck's Head** pub at Meonstoke, which I have often used of an evening. The 'buck' turns out to be a stag — quite a different sort of beast — if the stag's head on the sign is a guide, although a fallow buck's antlers over the door go at least part way to correct any misapprehension! Opening 1100-1430 and 1800-2300 on weekdays and the usual hours on Sundays. A good range of brews including traditional ales. Food served from 1200-1400 and 1900 to about*

Meonstoke village was swept by fire in the early 18th century and so retains few older buildings. Two thatched, brick-built barns maintained in an excellent state of repair look well in their village centre setting.

Walk 16

Distance: Allow 4 to 5 hours for this 8-mile walk.

From the village centre corner where a cul-de-sac leads to Droxford church, cross the main road and follow Park Lane westward, soon crossing Union Lane to continue along a narrower uphill byway leading past Droxford Primary School and a red-brick Scout Hut on your left. A footpath sign points your way ahead along a lane which becomes gravelled, and then grassed, with a fence to your left and a hedge and a recreation ground to your right. Arable land to your left and ahead is rimmed by rising chalkland, part-wooded and partly grass-sloped, as you approach a metal gate flanked by a stile. Here a sign says 'Private property, keep to footpaths, dogs on leads', despite which I soon met a walker whose dog was not on a lead.

The 'WW' logo and arrow here and subsequently signify that, at the start of this walk, you are following part of The Wayfarer's Walk (Emsworth to Inkpen Beacon, Berkshire). Beyond the metal gate a rising track leads along the right-hand edge of arable farmland, with a hedge and then just a fence to your right. Where the fence eventually turns right your now unfenced track dips to cross a curving valley, beyond which you climb again to a stile below a slope where winter-migrant fieldfares chack-chacked among treetops as I arrived here.

2130 ranges from sandwiches to lasagnes, grilled lamb chops, steaks, and choice of sweets. Vegetarian dishes available.

Having crossed the stile, you follow a path right-handed, out from under tall beeches and sycamores and along the foot of a grassy slope to a stile preceding more arable land. Your path now angles right to skirt the right-hand edge of this, with views across the Meon Valley to Old Winchester Hill, on your right, which is where the South Downs proper begin. At the field's end cross a stile by a metal gate with a wood-edge track leading on ahead. Ignore the latter and leave The Wayfarer's Walk at this point to turn left where a sign denotes an official footpath diversion, with a stile on the step of which I found a freshly-disgorged owl pellet consisting of undigested remains of some small prey.

Beyond the stile follow a rising wood-edge path, soon emerging on to the leftward margin of a grassy downland area. Follow the left-hand hedge and subsequent fence bounding this area, soon bending right and then left while enjoying magnificent right-hand views of chalkland flanking the Meon Valley. You then cross a stile and a lane to follow a signposted bridleway along the right-hand edge of an arable field, dipping towards a spinney along the crest of Shepherds Down. More superb views unfold here, across wide valley fields and woodlands to where Beacon Hill looms on the skyline.

Trees with trunks jacketed in ivy shade the bridleway which now leads you along the right-hand edge of the spinney overlooking Shepherds Down. Where trees thin out a fenced track leads on ahead between two pastures, then through more trees to where your bridleway joins another. Here you turn sharp right to head diagonally downhill. The tree-bordered track you now follow soon emerges on to a lane which you follow left-ahead. A hare raced across the field to my left as I approached a leftward bend of this lane, not many yards beyond which you turn right by a sign for Hazelholt Farm.

A farm road which is also a public footpath leads you past farm buildings, with white-walled Hazelholt mansion flanked by trees left-ahead as you continue along a track leading into woodland. Throwing up their heels to put on an impressive turn of speed, two roe deer fled into the wood from a neighbouring field as I headed north. As always, the sight of such lovely wild animals added pleasure to the walk.

Disregard signs indicating turnings right for Hazelholt Forest Products and carry on through the heart of the wood, passing a cottage on your left just before emerging through a gateway on to the Bishop's Waltham-Corhampton road. Cross the road to where a footpath sign points your way across a low fence and along a luckily well-used path which beats a course of its own through the crops on the ground that now lies ahead. In theory, farmers are required by law to reinstate paths after ploughing but all too many fail to do so, as I found to have been the case here.

Not far ahead you cross a stile, briefly rejoining The Wayfarer's Walk as you now turn right to follow a track along the south side of a wood called Bottom Copse. At the wood end, near the outbuildings of Steynes Farm, you join and follow left-handed the clearly-defined route of a bridleway leading into Bottom Copse, all other tracks and paths being plainly marked as 'private'. After zigzagging right and then left through beech woodland, you cross a grassy vista to reach a gate and cross a road. Go over the stile alongside the metal gate now in front of you to follow a hedged bridleway which soon enters Littleton Copse. 'F/p' signs keep you on track through this otherwise private wood, through which your path skirts the right-hand edge of a grassy glade to reach a T-junction of tracks. Turn right, then left, then right again where right of way signs indicate to leave the wood at its north-eastern corner, where I sat on a horse-jumping trestle to eat a belated picnic lunch.

With a thick hedge on your left, follow the leftward edge of the sizeable arable field that you now enter. At the end of it you reach and cross a road to follow a chalk-and-gravel hedged track downhill, with a dwelling to your right at the start of it. Hillside plantations and sheep-grazed pastures alternate alongside what in parts is a muddy trackway: a hollow lane of great antiquity which those who improved country byways for motoring did not think fit to include in their schedules. Beyond Exton Stud, a Georgian farmhouse on your right, the lane is metalled for the last few yards to its junction with another, which you follow ahead to where it soon bends left on the outskirts of Exton.

Turn right here alongside a flint-walled barn to follow a fenced grass path to a swing-gate, then along the right-hand edge of a paddock and through a gap into a second paddock with no intervening gate or stile. The tree-fringed River Meon curves to your left as you approach a second stile, beyond which you emerge past a house with herringbone brickwork in its structure to reach and follow left-handed a gravel drive below Corhampton church. Spare time to visit this Saxon-built place of worship and to marvel at the enormously old and massive churchyard yew before crossing the

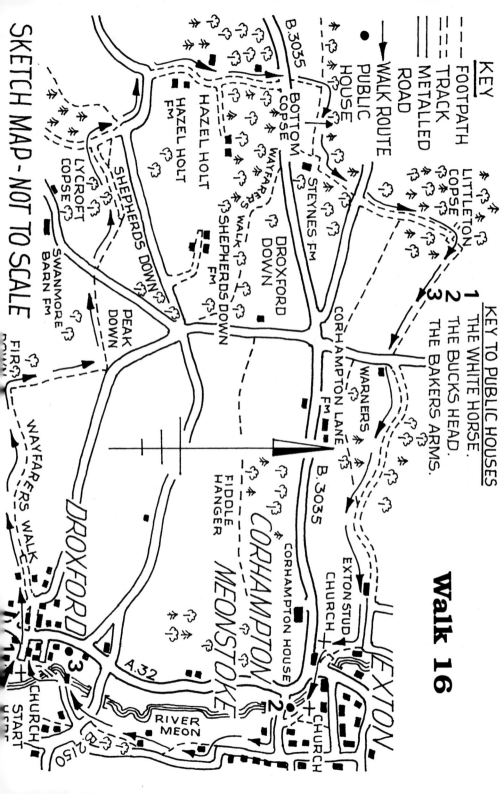

Walk 16

SKETCH MAP - NOT TO SCALE

KEY
- — — FOOTPATH
- = = = TRACK
- ═══ METALLED ROAD
- → WALK ROUTE
- ● PUBLIC HOUSE

KEY TO PUBLIC HOUSES
1 THE WHITE HORSE.
2 THE BUCKS HEAD.
3 THE BAKERS ARMS.

adjacent A32 and following it right-handed for a few yards to a River Meon fish weir.

Cross the river here by a footbridge and follow a path to Meonstoke churchyard entrance, just ahead. Although part of its structure dates from the 13th century, the most eyecatching feature of Meonstoke's Church of St. Andrew is its canopied tower. This dates from 1900 when the original tower, believed to have been built in the 15th century, needed repairs. Peeping out above surrounding greenery and set back a trifle, as it is, from the village it serves, the church is visually one of the Meon Valley's most appealing.

Follow the driveway leading out on to the road by The Buck's Head pub. Follow the road left-handed, then take the first turning right to head south through Meonstoke village centre. Most of the bordering houses are of 18th century vintage, having been built following a fire which devastated older dwellings. Two thatched, brick barns on your right are pleasing examples of old farm buildings which have been kept in sound structural order and are a credit to their owner.

Where the village road soon bends left, continue ahead along a driveway past Meonstoke Infants and First Year School, beyond which a fenced grass path leads ahead and then veers half-left across grass through scattered trees to a stile. Cross this to join and follow right-handed a tree-lined lane, not many yards along which a footpath sign points you right-handed along a gravel driveway. Bear left from this within a few yards to follow an earthen path through trees at the base of a steep bank on your left and with valley fields in view to your right. This bring you out past a house on to a driveway which you follow to joins the Droxford-Hambledon road, B2150.

Follow this left-handed for a few yards to some houses, then turn right to follow a narrow 'no through road', signposted as such. This heads downhill and ends at a footbridge where you cross the River Meon to follow a footpath to Droxford's old mill. Another footbridge crosses the mill race to reach the stub end of a cul-de-sac, where to your left you cross a stile to follow a path along the right-hand edge of a pasture. Leaving this via a kissing-gate, you join The Wayfarer's Walk for the third and last time and follow it right-handed through Droxford churchyard. Pause for a peep inside what Pevsner and Lloyd describe as 'a typically Hampshire village church'.

From the churchyard entrance follow the road for a very short distance to Droxford's main street and back to your car.

Woods and Water near Curbridge

WALK 17
At least **4 hours**
6 miles
Walk begins page 112

Background to the Walk

Curbridge lies in that narrow but precious green belt of countryside that separates Southampton's suburbs from the outer reaches of Fareham and Portsmouth. Coming upon it suddenly as a stranger passing through, you gain the impression of being deep in the heart of Hampshire, remote alike from towns and from the coast and its influences. Yet you only need peer over the bridge which spans the winding river here to realise that the sea makes a contribution to local geography, pushing tides upstream this far and bringing marine life into the area.

I once rowed all the way here from Hamble on a flood tide, stopped off at Botley for refreshment, then back again with the ebb tide to Hamble — and a very pleasant jaunt that was, if just a trifle hard on the hands. Romans and others did much the same, which doubtless explains a Roman building near the banks of the Hamble River, close to Curbridge. Right up to the First War, barges laden with coal and grain were poled up to Botley Mill, while the adjacent 'Botley Docks', so-called semi-seriously until well within living memory, recall a time when the tidal estuary was a conveyance for other merchandise.

The Curbridge estate is now National Trust property, and since 1968 the waterside woods west of the hamlet, through which the return stage of this walk leads, have been in the care of Hampshire and Isle of Wight Wildlife Trust, whose

Maps
Landranger 1:50,000
Sheet 196
Pathfinder 1:25,000
Sheets SU 41/51 and
SU 40/50
Map Reference of
Start/Finish SU527117

How to get there
From Southampton follow A3024 and A334 to and through Thornhill and Botley, just beyond which you turn right to follow A3051 for a mile to Curbridge. Solent Blue bus service 26 from Southampton via Hedge End to Bishop's Waltham connects at either Hedge End or Botley with buses on People's Provincial service 79 between Hamble and Fareham.

Pub facilities
The Horse & Jockey
Open weekdays between 1100-1500 and 1800-2300, except sometimes in summer when all-day opening is the rule to cater for

riverside walkers (usual hours on Sundays), the Horse and Jockey provides a full range of pub type food lunchtimes and evenings, seven days a week. Tuesdays - Saturdays an extended menu includes such items as salmon steak and chicken Kiev; Sunday roasts are available by prior booking. Old English recipes such as jugged hare and beef casserole are also featured. A supper licence enables drinks to be served with meals until midnight. Food may be ordered between 1200-1400 and 1830-2200.

leaflet, costing 10p, can be had from their headquarters. Just send a SAE (plus a small donation, if you like) to the Trust at 71 The Hundred, Romsey. The 24-acre reserve is bright with primroses, wood anemones, bluebells and Solomon's seal in spring, being carefully managed by coppicing to admit sufficient light to the woodland floor to stimulate plant growth. Among local specialities are specimens of the wild service tree, now rare elsewhere in Hampshire, while the estuary is a favourite haunt of wading birds, especially in winter.

For a place of such very modest size, one rather surprising thing about Curbridge is the presence here of a church. Dedicated to St. Barnabas, the little red-brick building under the trees beside the highway was built in 1892 as a daughter church of St. Paul's at Sarisbury and still has services every Sunday. Curbridge was briefly an independent parish, but owing to insufficient parishioners it was partitioned between Curdridge and Wickham, and so it remains.

Walk 17

Distance: Allow up to 4 hours for this 6-mile walk.

From The Horse and Jockey follow the twisting main road south, passing St. Barnabas Church on your left on your way to where a gravel road, marked 'private', diverges left into an oakwood. This is a public path, so follow it to where a footpath sign soon points your way ahead and the gravel road, now indeed 'private' even to walkers, bends to the left.

The narrow path, I am told, was once a coach road from Botley to Titchfield, though there is nothing today to show this. Looking at the map, one cannot help wondering why the road did not live on into the motoring age, so much more direct was it than the present A3051, which loops around by way of Burridge, Swanwick and Park Gate on its way towards Titchfield and Fareham. This fact has not been wholly lost sight of. There are plans to make a new road which will effectively cut corners — and which will certainly detract in no small measure from the tranquillity of the first part of this walk, so make the most of this while you may!

Ahead now lies a wilderness of wood and quiet meadow whose survival up to the present must almost be counted among modern miracles. Penetrating it gives a sense akin to exploring the unknown, and one of the marvels about this area is that so very few people do know it: another good reason for not wasting time if you want to make good such a deficiency while it is still truly worth the effort.

Flanking woodland is replaced by oaken strips on either hand through which weedy pastures can be seen as you head south along the footpath. Two ditches are spanned by planks, leading you dryshod — all being well — to a stile which you cross to enter a meadow straight ahead from where a hedged green lane turns left and another stile lies to your right. An ancient sign, 'Bew of B', was nailed high on an oak tree here when we passed. If, as must be assumed, this refers or once referred to the possible presence of a bull, we saw no sign of any such beast. The law allows bulls to be at large where there are public rights of way provided they are with cows and are not one of the dairy breeds, which are deemed more dangerous than beef breeds, though most walkers doubtless prefer not to put the matter to the test!

A line of oaks separates the meadow you now enter from another to your right as your path continues ahead to a plank over a ditch — one of the Hamble River's feeder streams — and your entry point to dense conifer woodland. 'Dogs on leads, please' requests a notice, emphasising the importance of never letting your pets run out of control when in the countryside.

Sawpit Copse extends to your right, followed by a tree screen between yourself and neighbouring farmland as a grass ride now leads you south-eastward to where you emerge past a vehicle barrier on to a gravelled forest road. Turn left to pass around another car barrier and follow the gravel road into a wood called Whiteley Pastures. Dense conifers on your left contrast with a wood of young oaks to your right as you now head north-east into the heart of a very extensive tract of forest. Wildlife I have seen here varies from foxes and shy roe deer to rare butterflies and adders, so it pays to keep your eyes skinned. If you do see an adder, ignore it and, above all, do not harm it, for these creatures are protected under Forestry Commission bye-laws and, in any case, are harmless so long as you do not handle or step on one.

After crossing a culverted stream, your gravel road angles slightly left as it climbs through a mixture of mainly dense conifers and broadleaved trees. At the crown of the high ground in Ridge Copse, as this part is called, leave the gravel to follow a clearly-defined path left-handed along the ridge, descending steadily through oaks to where a field comes into view through

The Hamble River from Curbridge Nature Reserve

trees to your right. Reaching a right-hand bend in the wood-edge where a broadish track keeps straight on, take a narrow path which turns right, keeping the wood-edge in view to your right until a right-hand twist of the path takes you over a plank and a stile to leave the wood by a very old oak tree.

Here you enter the grounds of Ridge Farm to follow the right-hand edge of a field with a hedgerow to your right. Just ahead now is the farmhouse, sadly derelict and deserted, a description no less applicable to the fields round about as we saw them. On the near side of the farmhouse turn left to follow a green lane hedged with scrub and then flanked by farmland after crossing a brick-parapeted stream culvert.

The green lane ends at a stile at a point where you cross your outward route within sight of the 'bull' sign, now to your left. Cross the stile ahead to follow the left-hand edge of a meadow with a tree hedge to your left. From the meadow's end follow a path fenced on the right from neighbouring ground, pushing on ahead through encroaching scrub to emerge on to an unmetalled lane. You can either follow this right-handed past scattered cabins and assorted outhouses to reach and head right along the main road towards the northern end of Burridge, or stick to the path by crossing the unmetalled road and ducking under a wooden bar there.

A fenced path now leads you alongside and then through a scrapyard to a miniature jungle of broom, where you skirt right of the thickest growth and then turn left, with a fence to your right, to join a path fenced on both sides. This leads past sheds and a caravan to a stile, beyond which an unmetalled lane brings you out on to the main road at Burridge a little way south of the alternative approach.

Head right-handed alongside the main road to where the metalled sidewalk ends just past Burridge Sports and Social Club premises. Now cross the road to follow a driveway hedged on the left and fenced on the right, leading into Curbridge Nature Reserve. At a track bend by a gate to

Walk 17

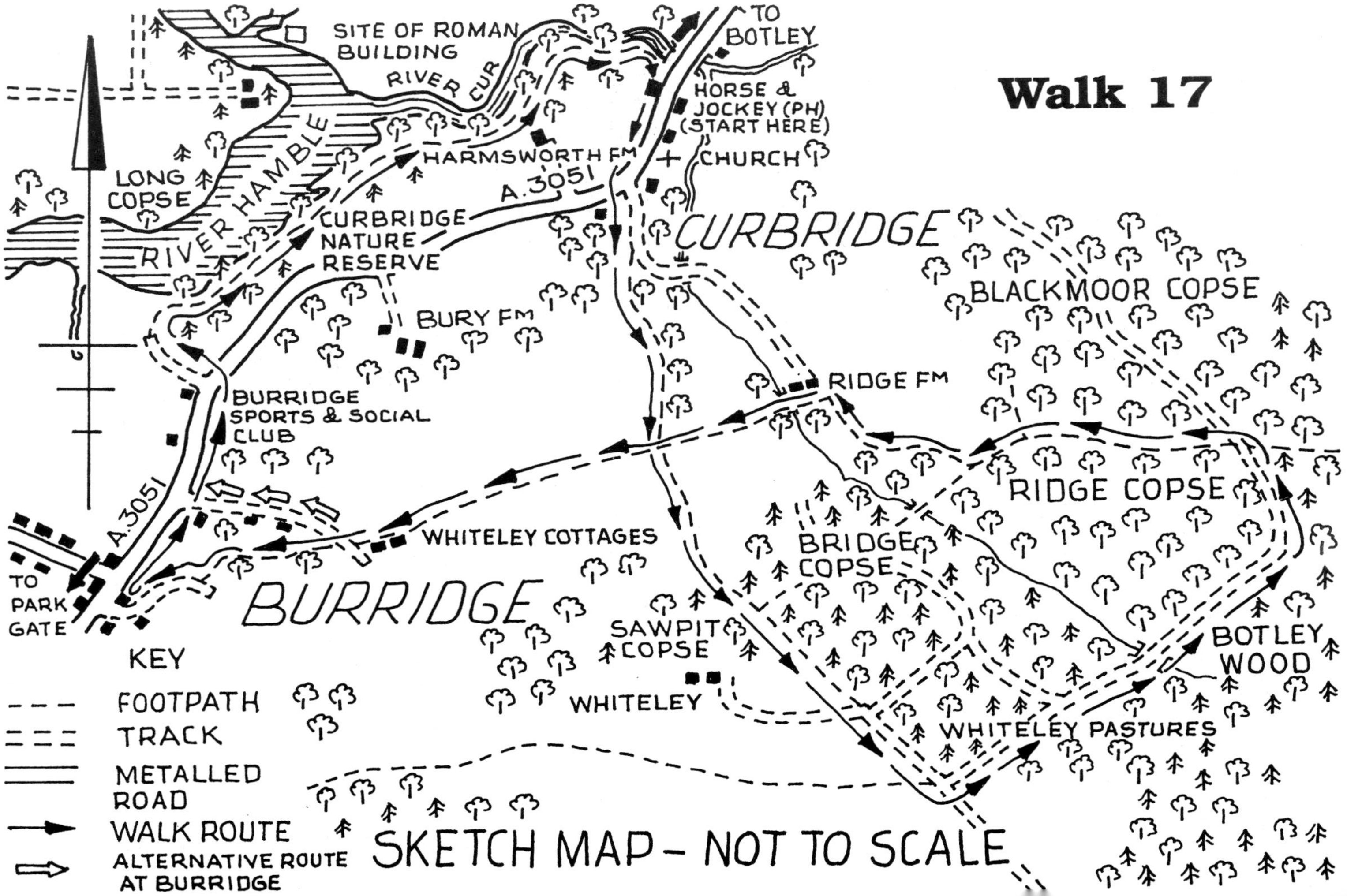

KEY

⇨	WALK ROUTE
→	ALTERNATIVE ROUTE AT BURRIDGE
———	METALLED ROAD
– – –	TRACK
··· ···	FOOTPATH

TO PARK GATE

A.305I

BURRIDGE SPORTS & SOCIAL CLUB

WHITELEY COTTAGES

BURRIDGE

WHITELEY

SAWPIT COPSE

BRIDGE COPSE

WHITELEY PASTURES

RIDGE FM

RIDGE COPSE

BOTLEY WOOD

BLACKMOOR COPSE

CURBRIDGE

BURY FM

CURBRIDGE NATURE RESERVE

A.305I

HARMSWORTH FM

CHURCH

HORSE & JOCKEY (PH) (START HERE)

TO BOTLEY

RIVER HAMBLE

LONG COPSE

SITE OF ROMAN BUILDING

RIVER CUR

SKETCH MAP – NOT TO SCALE

Stepped footpath, Curbridge Nature Reserve

your left, walk round a metal gate half-right of you and then head downhill to where the hedge beside you bends to the left. With the upper Hamble estuary spread panoramically before you, carry on down, with a wood on your right, to the bank of the river.

From here a path, stepped in places to help minimise erosion on steeper ground, takes you right-handed through the wood. At intervals there are seats ideally placed for enjoying a 'breather' while soaking up the sylvan scene and casting your eye across the river which complements the wood's charms so effectively. Glass-smooth water seen through the trees as we made our way through the reserve revealed a flock of Canada geese, very much at home on this English tideway — one of many British waters where these immigrants are nowadays almost too plentiful for comfort.

Threading your way along this timbered escarpment, which at several points has crumbled with trees lying prostrate in the river where time and tide have done their worst, you might be exploring a bit of Hampshire where the primeval past still lingers. Much loving care is needed to ensure its preservation as a scenic nature sanctuary second to none in southern Hampshire.

Presently you reach the point where the tideway bifurcates, one part of it winding on towards Botley while the other swings right-handed. This latter is what the county wildlife trust calls in its leaflet the 'River Cur', a name I have not seen mentioned elsewhere, though perhaps it will serve as well as any other for the creek alongside which, through bordering trees, your path now meanders east to Curbridge and the finish of your walk.

Down to the Sea from Titchfield

WALK 18
Allow **3** to **4 hrs**
6 miles
Walk begins page 119

Background to the Walk

Titchfield and the Meon Valley combine the visual attractions of one of Hampshire's most ancient townlets with those of a belt of rural greenery between great chunks of urban development which would otherwise coalesce. The river which gives the valley its name recalls that of a Jutish tribe, the Meonwara, who settled in the area not long after the Romans left Britain and whose conversion to Christianity coincided fairly closely with the building of Titchfield's first church. Parts of the structure of that building, dating from as far back as the seventh or eighth century, survive in the lower portion of the west tower of today's church.

The village name first appears as 'Ticcefelda' in an AD982 Charter of King Ethelred the Unready, and is thought to signify a field where goats were grazed, unless perhaps 'Ticce' was the name of some forgotten local worthy. Domesday Book calls it 'Ticefelle', records it as being held by the King in AD1086 and having a market and a mill. It also makes mention of 'Burnewic', present day Brownwich, held at the time by the Bishop of Winchester.

Between the years 1231 and 1537 Titchfield was the setting for a monastery of the Premonstratensian Order of White Canons, who built their abbey just north of the present A27. The vicar of Titchfield was one of their members, his parish extending over an area stretching from

Maps
Landranger 1:50,000 Sheet 196
Pathfinder 1:25,000 Sheet SU 40/50
Map Reference of Start/Finish SU537058

How to get there
From Southampton follow A3024 to Windhover roundabout and M27, from which take the Fareham West exit. Follow A27 towards Fareham and turn right where a sign points the way to 'Titchfield Village only'. Approaching the village centre from Southampton Hill, turn right at the signposted entrance to the free car park, where cars may be left for not more than three hours. Otherwise, unless using a pub car park, find roadside parking space in Southampton Hill or one of the other village roads where this is permissible. People's Provincial

buses on service 80
pass through Titchfield
en route between
Southampton and
Fareham, on service 77
between Fareham and
Warsash and service
72 between
Southampton and
Gosport.

*Right: Path to shore,
near Brownwich*

Pub facilities
The Bugle Hotel.
*This pub has a choice
of beers from around
the world and 100
whiskies as well as an
à la carte restaurant .
Food served lunchtimes
and evenings every
day, from 1200-1400
and again from 1900-
2200 (weekday pub
hours are 1100 to 1500
and 1800 to 2300,
Sunday opening as
usual). Pub walkers
may use the car park.
There is a family room.*
The Queen's Head
Hotel.
*This village inn has
turned its public bar
into a roomy restaurant
with an à la carte
menu lunchtimes and
evenings except
Sunday. Food ordering
from 1200 to 1400
daily and from 1900 to
2130, bar meals being
available at lunchtimes
and on all except*

beyond Wickham in the north to the Hamble River
in the west and the shore of the Solent in the
south. When Henry VIII dissolved the abbeys the
Titchfield property was given to Thomas
Wriothesley (pronounced 'Risley') who became
first Earl of Southampton. A memorial to members
of his family is the main feature of a chapel on the
south side of the chancel in the church as we see
it today.

Mediaeval Titchfield was a minor coastal port
lying at the head of a tidal inlet. This changed
when in 1611 Henry, third Earl of Southampton,
had a bank built across the mouth of the River
Meon, reclaiming the estuary, and a canal dug for
barge traffic upstream to Titchfield. The canal
lasted barely a century, its exit eventually being
sealed off.

Titchfield's Church of St. Peter is older by far in
part than any other local building. Originally a
minster church serving the surrounding area, its
size and spaciousness mirror its importance. Like
many another Hampshire church it was 'restored'
in the 1860s, not altogether sympathetically, but
it greatest treasure, the west tower, with its Anglo-
Saxon origin and splendid Norman doorway as
well as its 15th century broach-spire, has been
well looked after throughout the ages.

Walk 18

Distance: Allow 3 to 4 hours for this 6-mile walk: longer if you plan to dally by the sea.

From the free public car park approached by turning right from Southampton Hill after turning off the A27 for Titchfield village, follow the signposted footway between buildings to reach Titchfield High Street directly alongside The Queen's Head Hotel. Terraced shops and dwellings of various stiles, periods and numbers of storeys crowd both sides of the main thoroughfare as you follow it right-handed through the village centre for a short distance.

Opposite Church Street, with the ancient church facing you from the end of it, turn right to follow West Street. Parson's Cottages, on the left, bear a plaque relating them to the Earl of Southampton 1990 Trust, a name instantly recalling that of the nobleman into whose hands Titchfield Abbey and its lands passed after Henry VIII expropriated all monastic properties.

After passing the former West End Inn, turn left by Guessons Cottage to follow a macadamised path flanked by an ivy-crested wall of very obvious antiquity, incorporating herringbone brickwork. Watching me make notes a passer-by expressed the hope that my companion and I had no thoughts of despoiling this chunk of old-time Titchfield, at the same time drawing our attention, further west along West Street, to the 200 year-old 'knuckle-bone wall', embodying hundreds of sheep bones in its structure.

Ignore a path diverging right and carry on alongside a more modern brick wall to reach a road which you follow right, and then left along Lower Bellfield. Where the next road, Bellfield, turns right and Hewett Road diverges left you will have your first chance to glimpse the sea beyond the green valley left-ahead as you now follow a

Sunday evenings. Brews include Whitbread Traditional and a guest ale. B&B accommodation. Walkers using the pub may use the car park. **The Coach and Horses.** *At the junction of South Street, Bridge Street and Coach Hill, this is a typical local with good range of brews, including a guest beer, and a car park walkers may use if they ask first. Food is confined to cold snacks and notice is needed if large parties are to be catered for. Open weekdays between 1030-1430 and 1800-2300 and at the usual times on Sundays.* **The Wheatsheaf.** *A beer garden, a family room and a rear car park go with this small village pub in Titchfield's East Street. A temporary manager was in charge when I called. Traditional ales, full meals and snacks have been featured previously at this Courage house.*

path ahead. After making your way between private gardens and garages on Titchfield's outskirts you cross a green and an iron-railed stile into a pasture preceded by a public footpath sign.

Cattle here regarded us with a quizzical eye as we disregarded an ill-defined path heading diagonally right and followed the well-defined one straight ahead, squeezing under the metal bar top of a stile with a wire strand halfway up to follow the next section of the path, with a fence to the left and a tall hedge on the right. Beyond tree-bordered valley fields ahead the Isle of Wight looms on the skyline as Great Posbrook Farm and its outbuildings are passed on your right-hand side.

Cross a stile, a farm track and a second stile, where we found the step missing, to continue along the grassy left side of a long arable field. Your grass path joins a macadamised drive which you follow ahead, with a tree-surrounded market garden and a timber-framed cottage to your left. Where a sign on your left indicates the way 'to Lower Posbrook Farm only' follow a tarmac drive right-handed to join the Titchfield-Meon Shore lane where this bends right at Little Posbrook.

Triangle Lane, as this is called, leads you left-ahead and soon bends left to skirt Thatchers Coppice. Ignore a concrete road that turns right-handed into this, then after a few yards turn right into a public woodland car park. On the right-hand side of this is a notice suggesting that the little wood's name derives from its bygone purpose of growing hazel for use as thatching spars.

Thatchers Coppice forms part of a Hampshire County Council owned estate comprising farmland, woodland and wetland and forming a broad green coastal wedge between the Hamble and Meon Valleys. Conservation and public access are well catered for, the latter with footpaths including some especially created to enlarge the network of pre-existing rights of way.

One of these paths leads you right-handed through Thatchers Coppice before emerging from it to run parallel with the concrete road aforementioned. With a wide spread of arable farmland to your left, your path swings left when the road does the same at Little Brownwich. A subsequent right-hand bend takes you across the concrete road where a footpath sign now points your way along a stony track circuiting the walled and fenced private grounds of Brownwich Farm (pronounced 'Brunnidge').

Your path turns left with a leftward fence, then at the end of this twists right to tunnel through greenery and be joined by a path from your right before crossing the Brownwich Stream by a wooden footbridge. Oak branches lean out above you and a post-railed pony paddock spreads along rising ground to your left as you approach a second footbridge. A

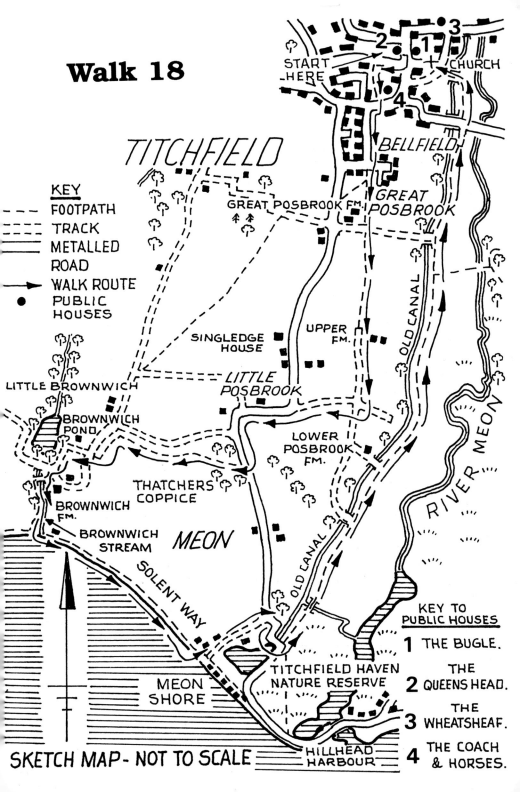

Walk 18

TITCHFIELD

START HERE

CHURCH

BELLFIELD

GREAT POSBROOK

GREAT POSBROOK FM.

KEY
- – – **FOOTPATH**
- – – **TRACK**
- ═══ **METALLED ROAD**
- → **WALK ROUTE**
- ● **PUBLIC HOUSES**

SINGLEDGE HOUSE

UPPER FM.

LITTLE POSBROOK

OLD CANAL

LITTLE BROWNWICH

BROWNWICH POND

LOWER POSBROOK FM.

THATCHERS COPPICE

BROWNWICH FM.

BROWNWICH STREAM

MEON

RIVER MEON

SOLENT WAY

OLD CANAL

MEON SHORE

TITCHFIELD HAVEN NATURE RESERVE

KEY TO PUBLIC HOUSES
1 THE BUGLE.

2 THE QUEENS HEAD.

3 THE WHEATSHEAF.

4 THE COACH & HORSES.

HILLHEAD HARBOUR

SKETCH MAP- NOT TO SCALE

gentle, brackeny descent brings you to footbridge number three, which you cross as you now turn left to follow a section of The Solent Way long distance coastal walk.

This rises from shoreside shingle, into which the Brownwich Stream is swallowed up before it joins salt water, to follow a gravel-and-clay clifftop which, like others elsewhere in Hampshire, suffers badly from erosion. A shimmering morning sea spread smoothly towards the Isle of Wight as we followed this quiet coastway, stopping often to savour the scene and, rather longer, for an early lunch.

Hedged presently on both sides, the coast path passes in front of two large houses before crossing a stile where Meon Shore's chalets begin. Here turn left to follow a path which becomes a drive bordered by trees, with Meonside marshland to your right. A gate and stile precede the metalled motor road which next leads you right-handed, twisting right and then left to cross by a little three-arched bridge the canal completed in AD1611 as a route for barge traffic to Titchfield.

After crossing the bridge turn left to follow a willow-bordered track which was once a towpath for barge horses. Beyond a stile, just ahead, the old canal, to your left, survives as a damp and rushy hollow framed by trees. This alters after you cross a concrete bridge spanning a westerly arm of the River Meon on the edge of Titchfield Haven Nature Reserve, a county council owned bird sanctuary around the outflow of a river which was once a tidal estuary reaching as far inland as Titchfield.

With water now spreading from bank to bank across the canal course alongside you, your tree-lined towpath skirts the edge of marshy meadowland before reaching another stile. Cross this and carry on through what we found as an open gateway, with a fence between yourself and Meonside pastures to your right, then through a second open gateway beyond which a gravel track matures briefly into a metalled road.

A pedestrian side access around a locked farm gate precedes a further gate and stile, followed in turn by two more gates with a narrow way around them for pedestrians. Having reverted to a mere path, your walking route next becomes a driveway leading out on to a road, which you cross to follow a hard-surfaced path beyond. We glimpsed trout in the shallows where a wooden footbridge takes you over the old canal. Your path now turns left to skirt Titchfield churchyard, then emerges in front of St. Peter's, with its partly pre-Norman western tower, to follow Church Street, bordered by picturesque old cottages, back into High Street. A right turn along this leads past The Bugle Hotel to The Queen's Head Hotel, on the near side of which you turn left for the public car park.

A Waterside Walk from Warsash

WALK 19
4 or 7 hours
3 or 5 miles
Walk begins page 124

Background to the Walk

Modern Warsash is no longer rural. It forms part of a semi-urban area which also embraces Sarisbury, Swanwick, Park Gate, Titchfield Common and Locks Heath, and is still growing in population. Until the early decades of the century this corner of south Hampshire was noted for strawberries rather than people, with Warsash having a special renown as a place to enjoy crab teas. Nowadays, yachts rather than crabs are its raison d'etre. A glance at the Hamble River estuary on a sunny weekend in summer makes it all too obvious why most people first think of the Hamble (with the possible exception of Cowes) as the south coast's number one centre for sailing.

The sea looms large in the life of Warsash in another important way, for here is the College of Maritime Studies where those whose working lives are concerned with the operation of merchant shipping receive their training. The college occupies a large area just to the south of Warsash proper, between Newtown Road and the Hamble River.

With so much new building in recent decades, one has to look hard for visual signs of the antiquity of Warsash. A record from 1272 refers to it as 'Weresasse', a name which is thought to derive from the presence of an ash tree, or trees, by a weir, or perhaps belonging to someone called Waer. The community as a whole is officially known as Hook-with-Warsash. The hamlet of

Maps
Landranger 1:50,000 Sheet 196 Pathfinder 1:25,000 Sheet SU 40/50 Map Reference of Start/Finish SU494062

How to get there
From Southampton follow A3024 eastwards to Windhover roundabout, A27 from there via Bursledon to Sarisbury Green, and there turn right to follow Barnes Lane, leading to Brook Lane which you follow right-handed to Warsash. Turn right at Warsash Square for the car parks at Warsash Shore. People's Provincial buses on services 72 and 73 between Southampton and Gosport pass through Warsash.

Pub facilities

With three pubs open all day from 1100- 2300 on weekdays and at usual times on Sundays, Warsash offers a good range of licensed facilities. The Rising Sun, facing the river, has no car park of its own. The free public car park opposite is often full but there is another just round the corner, to the right as you approach via Shore Road. Fish dishes a speciality & food can be ordered between 1200-1430 (until 1400 on Sundays) and between 1900-2130 (until 2100 on Sundays), with soup available all afternoon. Separate downstairs dining area, plus upstairs dining and drinking area seating 50. Traditional ales are Marston's Pedigree and Flowers' Original, and there is a skittle alley. A plaque on the outside wall recalls the part played by Warsash in preparation for D-Day landings in Normandy, and a memorial opposite commemorates the Allied Naval and Commando units which sailed from the Hamble River for France.

Hook lies a mile south-east and shares with Warsash a parish church which was built in 1871 and lies halfway between the two. The most intriguing structure in Warsash is the clock tower by the square. This was built as a water tower serving Warsash House, where Edward VII sometimes stayed but which has long since been demolished. Hook Park, a 19th century mansion between Warsash and the sea, was destroyed by fire, but the stabling survives and forms the focal point of a development of luxury dwellings overlooking Southampton Water where it joins the Hamble River.

Another local link with the past is Hamble Ferry, which has been operating for hundreds of years and is one of the few of its kind still to function. I remember it from my pre-World War II boyhood as having then been propelled by an oarsman who was less than happy at being asked to convey my bicycle as well as myself across the tideway from Hamble to Warsash. It is now a motorised affair and still in fairly brisk demand, especially during the summer months when the yachting fraternity's invasion is in full swing.

Walk 19

Distance: Allow 4 hours for this walk of just over 7 miles, or 3 hours for the 5-mile alternative.

I parked in Thornton Avenue, the first turning left from Crofton Way, which is the last turning right from Brook Lane before you reach Warsash Square when approaching from Southampton. As already indicated, the main car parks in Warsash are by the shore, reached by turning right at the square and heading downhill to the Hamble River. At the peak of the yachting season, however, the riverside car parks are often full so then you may have to look elsewhere. Assuming the square to be your starting point, pause for a wondering look at that clock tower, with its pebbledash exterior and curtained upper storey windows, before setting off on foot along Shore Road. Bracketed in its early stages by modern shops and houses of no particular distinction, this takes on something of the flavour of maritime, pre-suburban Warsash as it dips towards the river past a terrace of old dwellings with variegated rooflines.

The present day pulls you up with a jolt at Warsash Shore, where the car parks and their approaches compete for congestion on summer weekends with the pleasure craft-packed estuary of the Hamble River beyond. There must surely come a time when not a single extra fibreglass hull will find room on that tidal inlet!

Peace returns with surprising swiftness as you turn left by the three-storeyed Rising Sun pub, just opposite one of the car parks, to where tarmac gives way within yards to a gravelly path alongside the river. You are now on part of The Solent Way long distance walk, which leads between Milford-on-Sea and Emsworth and keeps as close to the coast as possible (which is not very close at some points where no rights of way are available). The path rises to follow the rim of an oaken bank with the river below before descending to pass between the tideway and the College of Maritime Studies.

After passing a jetty which probes out lengthily from the rear of the college complex, your sea wall path, as it has become, leads to a junction of paths by a vehicle barrier. Follow the path that leads right-handed over a causeway around an area of marsh to bridge the outflow of a brook called Hook Lake at the mouth of the Hamble River. When the tide is high, as it was when I did this walk, the fresh-water marsh on your left lies several feet below sea level. It is kept free from salt by a sluice which holds back the water in Hook Lake until the tide is once again low enough for gravity to empty it. The marsh forms part of Hook-with-Warsash Nature Reserve, a county council-owned wildlife

*Although its first landlord was apparently named Harry and was a man of ample proportions, **The Great Harry**, in Warsash Road just east of the square, is more likely to have been named after one of the warships in the Navy of Henry VIII! Either way, it is a friendly pub of the post-World War II era with three bars and a sizeable car park which walkers are welcome to use. Newly refurbished, this is very much a 'local' which attracts visitors and offers live music in the evenings on Thursdays and Sundays. Home-made hotpots, curries and chillies are typical items on a lunchtime menu which changes daily, food being available between 1200-1400 but not in the evening. Children welcome for meals. A Courage house offering three traditional ales. Function room available for conferences and parties.*

*Also in Warsash Road is **The Silver Fern**, named after the emblem of the All Blacks rugby team from New Zealand, its*

first landlord having been a 'Kiwi'. Another post-World War II arrival on the scene, this comfortable pub has an extensive bar area enabling customers to enjoy their drinks in a quiet corner. Traditional ales, two draught stouts, darts, pool and a children's play area are available, and there is a large garden with swings and a 'bouncing castle'. There is normally a choice of seven hot dishes as well as bar snacks, sandwiches and a children's menu as well as 'specials'. Food can be ordered between 1200-1415 and between 1800-2015 (from 1900 on Sundays). Walkers may use the pub car park, at their own risk.

sanctuary which the public are asked not to enter. To help enforce this a protective channel of water has been created along the shore side of the reserve once you have passed the long spit of shingle which marks the point where the Hamble estuary and Southampton Water meet.

In keeping with the shore alongside it, your path is partly of shingle as it continues between the nature reserve and the tideway of what is still Southampton Water until you reach a point parallel with Calshot Spit, where The Solent begins. This lower extremity of Southampton Water's eastern shoreline is surprisingly remote, its unspoilt rurality very strikingly in contrast with the industrial scene opposite, where Fawley Refinery and Fawley Power Station's chimney dominate the view. Things may not always have been so peaceful, for the Pathfinder map reminds us of the one time presence here of a saltworks for extracting salt from sea water by evaporation and boiling.

In summer, if you have thoughts about combining your walk with a swim, you will be wise to find out beforehand if the tide will be high. The water is otherwise rather muddily inaccessible. Watch out for tarry deposits of oil on any beach shingle where you may sit — I paid the price for not taking this simple precaution one summer recently when I swam here. The sheer volume of plastic flotsam which accumulates here in summer also helps to give this shoreline a low rating for bathing.

A wire fence flanks your path as you continue to where erosion has attacked the footway proper and forced a diversion on to the beach. Where the path resumes you follow the top of a low cliff to Solent Breezes Holiday Centre, a complex of chalets and residential caravans which forces a further diversion of what was originally a coast path all the way along this shore. Except when the tide is really high you can walk along the beach below the site's protective wire-and-boulder walling as far as some wooden steps leading left-handed past the Solent Breezes office. From this a tarmac path or road takes you right-handed to where a gravel track continues to a stile at the end of the site, where you resume the coast path proper.

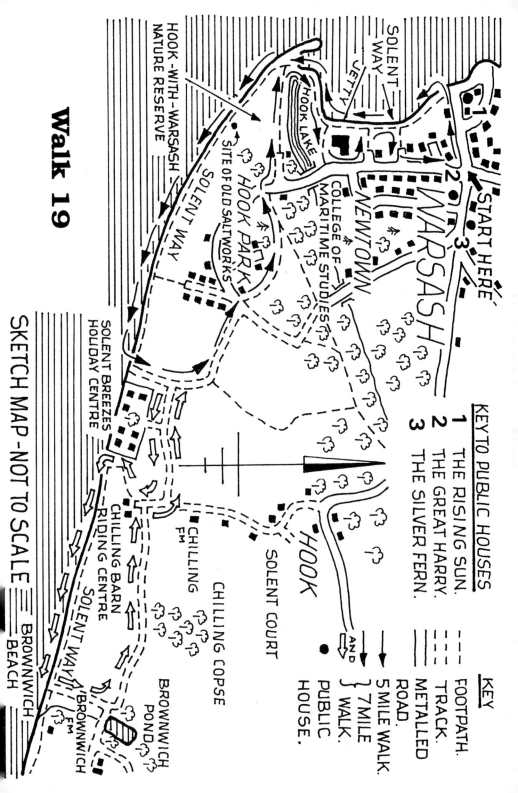

Walk 19

SKETCH MAP - NOT TO SCALE

KEY TO PUBLIC HOUSES

1 THE RISING SUN.
2 THE GREAT HARRY.
3 THE SILVER FERN.

KEY

FOOTPATH. -------
TRACK. - - -
METALLED ROAD. ——
5 MILE WALK.
7 MILE WALK.
PUBLIC HOUSE. ●

START HERE

WARSASH

SOLENT WAY

JETTY

HOOK LAKE

NEWTOWN

COLLEGE OF MARITIME STUDIES

HOOK - WITH - WARSASH NATURE RESERVE

HOOK PARK

SITE OF OLD SALTWORKS

SOLENT WAY

SOLENT BREEZES HOLIDAY CENTRE

CHILLING BARN RIDING CENTRE

SOLENT WAY

CHILLING FM

CHILLING

CHILLING COPSE

SOLENT COURT

HOOK

BROWNWICH POND

BROWNWICH FM

BROWNWICH BEACH

*Clifftop path near
Brownwich*

Otherwise, at the start of Solent Breezes turn left, past a vehicle barrier, to follow a tree-lined gravel lane inland for a few hundred yards. Where a stile confronts you the unmetalled byway turns right to pass the entrance to the chalet site, leading on to a junction of gravel lanes where you turn right, through a gate, to head towards Chilling Barn Riding Centre. Approaching another gate, turn left to a vehicle barrier, directly beyond which you follow a right-turning footpath. This skirts the grounds of the riding centre and is paralleled by a bridleway as it takes you around the right-hand edge of a field back to the clifftop.

From here two parallel paths head south-east: a continuation of the bridleway, fenced from the farmland to your left, and a footpath, close to the cliff, which later merges with the bridleway for a short distance before resuming its separate course. Cliff erosion is all too apparent here, making it necessary for the coastal right of way to have been re-routed a few yards farther from what used to be the cliff edge. Hampshire County Council owns the farmland hereabouts and has been able to make the necessary provision to maintain access for walkers and riders along this stretch of the county's shoreline.

Ahead lies the beach at Brownwich, where I paused to eat lunch. It was a sunny day just before Christmas, with walkers out and about in large numbers. Also much in evidence were winter-migrant brent geese, a large flock of which settled briefly on the water just off the coast here before departing as a murmurous throng for pastures not far inland.

On the near side of the stream outflow at Brownwich beach turn left to head inland along a gravel road fenced on the left and with scrub flanking the stream valley to your right. This brings you to a junction of gravel roads where a brief right-handed diversion is rewarded by a view of tree-surrounded Brownwich Pond, on which a solitary coot was the only water bird to be seen when I tried this walk. Otherwise, turn left at the gravel road junction to head back north-west between arable fields, passing Chilling

Copse on your right a few hundred yards before again reaching the vehicle barrier just east of the entrance to Chilling Barn Riding Centre.

Retracing part of your outward route in reverse, after passing the vehicle barrier turn right with the gravel road to a junction of unmetalled byways almost immediately ahead. Turn left here to follow the westerly gravel road back past the entrance to Solent Breezes Holiday Centre, keeping straight on where a sign points the way ahead to a 'public beach'. Trees which lean away from prevailing winds blowing off the sea intermittently flank the gravel road, and where this soon bends left cross a stile on your right to follow a green lane. Within a very short distance this becomes gravelled and bends left by where a footpath sign points across a field to your right.

Ignore the footpath and stay with the gravel road, from which the sea is in view across fields to your left. Where the gravel road next bends left cross a stile ahead to follow a path along the left-hand edge of a grass field. Cross the next stile, within sight of a rugby football pitch to your right, to follow the left-curving edge of the next field to an exit by the leftward of two footpath signs within view here. Now follow a driveway past some large houses on the fringe of the Hook Park development to join the principal road which serves this area. Follow this right-handed, downhill into the valley through which flows the stream called Hook Lake. Take the last driveway turning left before you would otherwise reach the bridge over this brook. Cross a stile by the last house bordering this driveway to follow a tree-lined causeway path alongside Hook Lake and the marshes of Hook-with-Warsash Nature Reserve.

Reaching the shore path at the mouth of the Hamble River, follow this right-handed over the sluice at the mouth of Hook Lake to the vehicle barrier at the end of the subsequent causeway. At the footpath junction here turn right to follow a tree-fringed gravel path around the edge of the area occupied by the College of Maritime Studies. This brings you into Newtown Road, which you follow left-handed, north, to the next public footpath sign on your left. Turn left here to follow a driveway to a vehicle barrier on your right, preceding another tree-shaded path which angles down once more to the river. Again, follow the shore path right-handed, and either stay with it to end your walk at one of the car parks near The Rising Sun, or else turn right within a very few yards to follow an earthen path through brambles and then re-emerge by way of another driveway into Newtown Road. Follow this left-handed to end your walk at or near Warsash Square.

Along Two Sides of the Hamble Estuary

WALK 20
Up to **4** or **5 hours**
6 or **7·5 miles**
Walk begins page 132

Background to the Walk

People mis-spell and mispronounce Bursledon often enough today to make it likely that it must have been a factor in frequent name changes in times past. Bussleton, Burtlesden, Bristelden and Brixenden have all found favour at different periods, no doubt as variants of Brixendona or Brixedone, as it was known over 800 years ago — there is still a Brixedone Farm in the parish. It may all have begun with a character called Beorhtsige having had something to do with a hill here, perhaps the one on which a windmill has stood since 1767. A successor erected in the year before Waterloo continued to work throughout most of the 19th century and has recently been restored — you will see it to your left from the A27 just after passing Windhover roundabout. Older by far is Bursledon's Church of St. Leonard, a legacy of a Bishop of Winchester's gift of land at Hamble to monks from France, who seemingly were required in return to build a place of worship for parishioners of 'Brixendona'. Despite the inevitable 19th century restoration, including enlargement, the 13th century chancel arch and some other relics of Early English structure have been preserved.

From at least the 14th to the early 19th century Bursledon was a centre for naval shipbuilding. Nelson's flagship at the Battle of Copenhagen, the Elephant, was a local ship whose name endures as one of the boatyards catering for today's

Maps
Landranger 1:50,000
Sheet 196
Pathfinder 1:25,000
Sheet SU 40/50
Map Reference of
Start/Finish SU489096

How to get there
From Southampton follow A3024 east to Windhover roundabout and A27 from there to Bursledon. Past The Swan, on your right just short of the railway bridge, turn right into Church Lane and then left into Station Road for the free car park by Bursledon station. For The Fox and Hounds, half a mile along A27 beyond Windhover roundabout turn right to follow A3025 into Lowford. Turn left by Lowford Car Sales to follow School Lane and turn right from this to follow Kew Lane, along which take the next right-hand turning immediately preceding the pub. Stopping trains

between Southampton and Portsmouth call at Bursledon, which is passed through by People's Provincial buses on services 71, 72, 78A and 80 (71 only on Sundays) from Southampton to Gosport or Fareham via Woolston and Lowford, and services 77A, 78, 78B and 80A (77A only on Sundays) from Southampton to Fareham via Bitterne and Windhover.

Pubs facilities
The Jolly Sailor.
Famous as a setting for the recent TV series Howards' Way, this riverside pub at Bursledon is directly accessible only on foot or by water — but well worth the effort. At both lunchtimes and evenings you can eat and drink in a friendly, old world atmosphere right alongside the yacht-thronged estuary.
The Swan.
Open from 1100-2300 seven days a week, this Bursledon hostelry is primarily a food pub with an extensive bar and restaurant menu. A restaurant licence

yachtsmen. The old-time 'wooden walls' largely depended on local timber for their construction, and there once was plenty of this near Bursledon. Important too were ironworks to provide essential fastenings, and Hungerford Bottom, where the Fox and Hounds pub is now, once echoed to the clangour of this industrial activity.

Latter-day population growth has helped create two very different Bursledons. Although map-makers seem reluctant to acknowledge it, by common consent the older dwellings strung alongside the maze of hilly byways south of the A27 and A3025 constitute a distinct community called Old Bursledon: a backwater which, because its lanes lead nowhere, retains the peace of a bygone age.

Hamble, although a backwater in the geographical sense, has sacrificed the benefits of physical isolation from the great wide world beyond to the needs of those who go sailing for pleasure. Before the 20th century brought not only yachtsmen but aircraft construction factories and an oil depot, this was a quiet fishing village where life went on at a leisurely pace and visitors were few. Long, long before that, its secluded situation was seen as ideal for the establishment by the Benedictine Order of a priory as a cell of an abbey in France. The necessary arrangements were made early in the 12th century by Bishop William Giffard of Winchester. Hamble's Priory Church of St. Andrew had its beginnings at that time, and retains much Norman handiwork, although parts of its original structure may have been moved around during subsequent alterations to the building, which I found locked when I tried this walk.

A notice in front of the church identifies it with 'Hamble-le-Rice', a name by which the community was first known in the 14th century — or so Nicolas Robinson tells us in his book *Hamble: A Village History*. Hamble is said to derive from 'hamel', meaning 'crooked' and referring not, I gather, to the character of those who at one time lived here but to the physical conformation of the river alongside it. 'Rice', Robinson links with an Old English word meaning 'brushwood', although others suggest it refers to the 'rise' or promontory of land upon which the village is located between the river and Southampton Water.

Walk 20

Distance : Allow four-and-a-half hours for the seven-and-a-half-mile walk or three-and-a-half hours for the 6-mile version.

Assuming a start at the public car park by Bursledon station, from the opposite side of the car park to the railway follow a steeply-rising macadamised path to the road above. Reaching this where it forks, bear left to cross a railway bridge. Follow the road for a short distance to where a stepped path descends left-handed, through trees, to The Jolly Sailor pub. Seats under a yew by the pub will tempt you to pause for refreshment while enjoying the river view here.

A path branching left from the one you descended takes you back to the road above, a cul-de-sac leading you left-handed to its end by a mini-foreshore close to a bend of the Hamble estuary: another view-spot. Then walk back along the cul-de-sac and over the railway bridge crossed previously, beyond which you fork left to follow a lane rather quaintly called High Street — perhaps the quietest in Hampshire. You are now in the heart of Old Bursledon, which is not so much a village as a random scattering of dwellings among gardens, trees and fields on hilly land overlooking the water.

A gate on the left-hand side of High Street gives access to a vantage point for a panoramic view embracing pastures sloping down to where the railway is backed by trees. This sylvan strip flanks a tract of tidal wetland called Hackett's Marsh,

enables drinks to be served with meals at any time. Family meals including Sunday three-course lunches are a speciality. Cars may be left in the large car park subject to prior permission.
The Vine Inn.
A small pub in the quiet heart of Old Bursledon, serving good food at lunch-times and evenings, except Sunday evenings, and open all day Saturday. Car parking space is limited.
The Fox and Hounds.
Hidden away in Hungerford Bottom at Old Bursledon, this popular pub's special feature is The Lone Barn, a beamy building of great character once located in a remote part of central Hampshire and now a roomy bar with excellent restaurant facilities and a large, open log fireplace. Many pub walkers already use the pub car park and others are welcome. Other pubs en route are **Ye Olde Whyte Harte**, **The Victory**, **The King and Queen** *and* **The Bugle** *at Hamble, and* **The Spinnaker** *at Lower Swanwick, all of which serve food.*

The Hamble River, looking upstream from Old Bursledon

with the curving estuary beyond. Hackett's Marsh is an undeveloped stretch of particular value as a sanctuary now that so much of the Hamble River south of Bursledon is occupied by marinas.

The Vine Inn lies on your left as you continue to where Salterns Lane, another cul-de-sac, bears left. For the slightly shorter walk disregard this and keep to the road which heads right-handed. Otherwise, follow Salterns Lane downhill to where it bends right and a gravelly track preceded by a footpath sign leads left-ahead. The latter takes you over a railway arch to a gateway to private property, from the near side of which a path flanked by oaks and hollies descends left-handed to end at a gate, with riverside marshland just beyond.

This path, although a blind alley, is worth exploring as a sample of the many little-known footways lacing the fields and lanes of Old Bursledon. For a second such exploration, retrace your steps to Salterns Lane and follow this left-handed to its end, from which a stony leftward path leads you downhill, under the railway by a brick arch, and then on along a low ridge called The Mound. Flanked by oozy creeks where once were pans for extracting salt from sea water by evaporation — perpetuated in memory by the name of Salterns Lane — The Mound today is a placid wilderness where scrubby oaks and furze escort the path to its saltmarsh conclusion.

Once again, return the way you came, pausing en route to take in the view across the creek to your left towards Badnam Copse, on its far bank, before heading back under the railway and up the hill to Salterns Lane. Follow this lane back to its beginning and there turn left to follow Kew Lane. If by now you are thirsty, stay with Kew Lane to a point just past where a right-hand footpath joins it and then follow a leftward path downhill through trees. Ahead lies Hungerford Bottom, and the building nestling in it, just to your right, is The Fox and Hounds. To reach this, turn right when you reach the next road. The Lone Barn lies just round the corner from the main building of the pub. Resuming your walk, follow the road by the pub downhill to where it forks by a 'no through road' sign and turn right there to follow a track merging with a footpath which leads you right-handed.

If you are giving this pub a miss, from Salterns Lane follow Kew Lane to the left, as already directed. Then, within yards, alongside a tile-roofed dwelling rather strangely called Thatched Cottage, turn left through a vehicle barrier to follow a fenced and hedged path downhill. This brings you to the end of another blind lane, which you cross to continue downhill along a path soon joined from the right by the track that forks right from the lane heading south from The Fox and Hounds.

The alternative routes reunite as you follow a gravel path right-handed of a house to a concrete stream bridge, which you cross. Your well-defined path now climbs fairly steeply through a northern continuation of the Badnam Copse you saw earlier from The Mound. Oaks and hollies shade your approach to a junction of paths at the top of the incline, where you bear left. A little way along here I sat on the fallen branch of a crabapple tree to eat my lunch while enjoying a woodland view essentially unchanged since the whole of the countryside hereabouts was ancient forest.

Your path soon joins a concrete track which you cross diagonally right-handed to follow a fenced path around the right-hand edge of ground securely wired off from public access. Part-metalled, part-gravelled, the path you are now following bridges the railway before reaching Satchell Lane. Named after a 13th century knight and landowner, one Sir Henry Shatershall, this winding but busy byway was once the only way into Hamble by road. Follow it left-handed to where it soon takes a leftward bend, a little way beyond which you follow a fenced footpath to your right. With a recently-planted hedge at first on the left and the old Hamble Airfield to your right, this path heads south to pass to the rear of houses flanking Satchell Lane.

At a junction of paths behind these houses, keep right-ahead to join and follow a road flanked by modern development to reach Hamble Lane

BURSLEDON

LOWER SWANWICK

HUNGERFORD BOTTOM

CHURCH

STATION (START HERE)

KEY
- - - FOOTPATH.
- - - TRACK.
——— METALLED ROAD.
→ WALK ROUTE.
⇨ LONGER ROUTE.
● PUBLIC HOUSE.

VIEW FROM HERE

HACKETT'S MARSH

RIVER HAMBLE

BROOKLANDS FM

THE MOUND

BADNAM COPSE

RAILWAY

Walk 20

KEY TO PUBLIC HOUSES
1 THE JOLLY SAILOR.
2 THE SWAN.
3 THE VINE INN.
4 THE FOX & HOUNDS.
5 YE OLDE WHYTE HARTE.
6 THE VICTORY.
7 THE KING & QUEEN.
8 THE BUGLE.
9 THE SPINNAKER.

HAMBLE

CHURCH

HAMBLE QUAY

WARSASH

FERRY

SKETCH MAP—NOT TO SCALE

directly opposite Hamble church. Hamble Lane becomes High Street as you follow it left-handed, passing Ye Olde Whyte Harte on your right as you approach the village square. From this you head right-handed down the picturesque lower High Street where it twists between old houses, shops and The Victory and The King and Queen pubs. As if two pubs in such a short distance were not enough, there then comes The Bugle, much favoured by leisure sailors and proud to have hosted such notabilities as ex-Prime Minister Ted Heath among other distinguished yachtsmen.

The Bugle lies opposite Hamble Quay, between which and the famous pub you follow the road right-handed. Where the road takes another twist to the right you carry straight on for Hamble Ferry, having made sure to reach it before 1730 on a weekday or 1600 on a Saturday or Sunday, after which times the ferryman is likely to have gone home! There are records of a ferry here as far back as 1493. In recent times it was owned by Watneys. When Watneys became part of Grand Metropolitan the ferry was sold to the current ferryman, Ray Sedgwick, who has been operating the service to and from Warsash since 1957.

The ferry shuttles between two hards which Mr. Sedgwick has to maintain. The ferry itself is an open boat devoid of weather protection. Ashore at Warsash, follow left-handed the gravel causeway path restored by the County Council a few years ago to make it possible once again to walk the east bank of the river to Lower Swanwick. For about half of its length there is water, or mud, on both sides of the walkway, with culverts and, at one point, a timber bridge to allow the tides to run in and out of those parts of the estuary east of the causeway which are otherwise cut off.

An earth path flanked by shingle well above water except at really high tides continues from where the first causeway ends and another soon begins. Beyond the end of the second causeway your footpath picks its way through a boatyard a little way short of Brooklands Farm, immediately past which the foreshore shingle can be bypassed by a parallel raised path when high tides make this necessary. Carry on from this to skirt a car park and then follow Swanwick Shore Road past some cottages before joining the A27 at Lower Swanwick, by Moody's boatyard. Turn left to pass The Spinnaker pub on your right and cross Bursledon Bridge. You then pass under the railway and turn left by The Swan to follow Church Lane for a short distance before turning left from this into Station Road to the station car park.